David O. McKay

AROUND THE WORLD

President Hugh J. Cannon and Elder David O. McKay

David O. McKay
AROUND THE WORLD

An Apostolic Mission

Prelude to Church Globalization

by
HUGH J. CANNON

spring creek
BOOK COMPANY
Provo, Utah

ISBN 13: 978-1-932898-
ISBN 10: 1-932898-
e. 1

Published by:
Spring Creek Book Company
P.O. Box 50355
Provo, Utah 84605-0355

www.springcreekbooks.com

Cover design © Spring Creek Book Company
Cover design by Nicole Cunningham

Printed in the United States of America
10 9 8 7 6 5 4 3 2 1
Printed on acid-free paper

Library of Congress Cataloging-in-Publication Data

Cannon, Hugh J. (Hugh Jenne), 1870-1931.
  David O. McKay around the world : an apostolic mission : prelude to church globalization
/ Hugh J. Cannon.
      p. cm.
  Includes index.
  ISBN-13: 978-1-932898-46-0 (pbk. : alk. paper)
  ISBN-10: 1-932898-46-8 (pbk. : alk. paper)
  1. Church of Jesus Christ of Latter-day Saints--Missions. 2. Mormon Church--Missions. 3.
McKay, David Oman, 1873-1970. 4. Cannon, Hugh J. (Hugh Jenne), 1870-1931. I. Title:
David Oman McKay around the world. II. Title.

BX8661.C36 2005
266'.9332--dc22
                    2005022259

ACKNOWLEDGMENTS

Inasmuch as the author and his wife are deceased, we their children have been privileged to work together in the preparation of this manuscript for publication. We are extremely grateful that this historic missionary journey was recorded for our benefit and for posterity.

We appreciate the time and effort of Katrina Cannon, a great-granddaughter of the author and his wife. Katrina converted the original typed manuscript with numerous handwritten additions and corrections to an electronic copy suitable for publication. She also assisted with other editing functions.

We express appreciation to Bill Slaughter and others at the LDS Church Archives for their help in providing some of the pictures.

The advice given by Cory Maxwell, Debby Simmons, and others at the Deseret Book Company has been very helpful.

We sincerely appreciate the assistance of Chad Daybell and his staff at Spring Creek Book Company for their valuable advice, editing, and cover design.

George. R. Cannon
Alice Cannon Hicken
Max R. Cannon
Dean R. Cannon

CONTENTS

ILLUSTRATIONS

PREFACE

Before he became Church President, Heber J. Grant recognized that many congregations had never seen a General Authority and worse, the Church did not understand their unique problems. At that time a solution to the unfortunate situation was not evident. The missions in America and Europe were visited often by the General Authorities. But the members in the Pacific and the Armenians in Syria were not so fortunate.

In October 1920 Elder David O. McKay was formally called by President Heber J. Grant to visit the missions of the Pacific and probably to go around the world. Hugh J. Cannon, a son of George Q. Cannon and the Liberty Stake President, was selected to accompany him. This was the first time an Apostle would travel so extensively. They made a year-long tour (December 4, 1920 to December 23, 1921) of LDS missions and other countries as they circumnavigated the world.

Their major goal was to visit missionaries and Church members and to stabilize their spiritual values. They also wanted to see what the various areas needed.

The two special missionaries visited the Orient: Japan, Korea, and China. On January 9, 1921, Elder McKay dedicated and set apart the land of China for the preaching of the gospel when missionaries are allowed to proselyte in that huge land.

Considerable time was spent in the missions of the Pacific Islands: Hawaii, Tahiti, Fiji, Tonga, Samoa, New Zealand, and Australia. The missionaries then traveled on to Java, Singapore, Burma, India, Egypt, Palestine, and Syria, where they met with about seventy

Armenian Saints who were without other missionaries and contact with the Church.

They returned home by way of Italy, Switzerland, Germany, Belgium, France, and England. During this tour of areas with little direct contact with the Church, they met with the missionaries and members in fifteen missions, two-thirds of the existing missions at that time. The only missions they did not visit were Canada, Mexico, Norway, Sweden, South Africa, and three in the United States. They experienced numerous spiritual experiences during their travels.

Elder McKay asked Brother Cannon to record their experiences, which he did. A serialized travelogue was published in the *Deseret News* as the letters arrived from various parts of the world. But the desire was to produce a more comprehensive narrative, including the spiritual episodes. Brother Cannon wrote an interesting twenty-five chapter account of the McKay/Cannon missionary journey. His work was interrupted by a call to serve as mission president for three years and other important activities. He died as it was nearing completion.

Speaking at Brother Cannon's funeral, Elder McKay said: "The narrative part of that wonderful mission has been printed in part in the *Deseret News*. Part of it has been printed in one of the European Church papers, but the spiritual side of it now may never be told because Brother Cannon was the one who could best tell it. That is one of many reasons why I say I wish that death had postponed this for many many years, for he and I have sat together since coming home and have planned ways and means of getting some of these memorable experiences in which God's power was manifest beyond the question of a doubt, to the young people of the Church, that their faith too might be increased."

Brother Cannon had discussed the details of the manuscript and his proposed additions with his wife, Sarah Richards Cannon, daughter of George F. Richards. She had been associate editor of an LDS University magazine and then a librarian at the university for several years, so she was uniquely qualified to assist him in writing, editing, and attempting to complete his document. After Hugh died,

Sarah completed and corrected the manuscript. With the renewed encouragement of President McKay, she then gave the manuscript to a publisher to be printed. Unfortunately, the publisher misplaced it, and it was not found for many years.

Now, eighty-four years after the important missionary world tour of Elder McKay, the lost manuscript has been published. It contains interesting and inspirational stories about the countries visited and the experiences of the two missionaries.

We wish the readers a hearty *bon voyage* as they undertake an imaginary tour around the world as it was back in 1921 in company with two faithful disciples of the Lord.

CHAPTER 1

CALLED TO SERVE

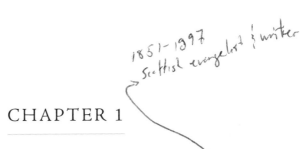

"It is the man who is the missionary. It is not his words.
His character is his message."

—Henry Drummond

We need your company, friends. Coleridge voiced a universal truth when he said, "What no one with us shares, seems scarce our own: we need another to reflect our thoughts." That conception followed to its conclusion is one of the great reasons for missionary work.

Come with us, therefore, on our trip around the world. If you join us in our experiences, you will sail tempestuous, also placid seas, many of them terrifying, others dreamy and restful. You will go into strange lands, some, comparatively, not yet out of their swaddling clothes, others falling into senility. You will be delighted with colorful Japan, awed by somber China, captivated by the "Come Back Land" of Hawaii, brought to tears by other hospitable South Sea Islands, including New Zealand and the continent of Australia, interested by over-populated Java, entranced by mystic India, inspired by historic Egypt, subdued and unfortunately incensed by holy Palestine. Naturally the temptation to linger unreasonably long in some of these lands must be resisted.

You will be strictly an "uncommercial traveler," seeking neither sales nor business opportunities, and yet it is not to be a pleasure

1

trip. You are to meet new peoples—not in a mere casual sense, but a feeling of intimacy so strong will be engendered that those of other races, other language, color, and customs will come to you and lay bare their hearts with the confident freedom of lifelong friends. It will be your duty to study their spiritual and, as far as possible, temporal needs, and to ascertain the effect of "Mormonism" upon their lives. Though your journey is westward, in due time eastern lands will be reached, whence all that is mystical as well as much that is true in religion has come.

Utah has an "Around the World Club" with a remarkably large membership, many of her citizens having encircled the globe. Still the journey you are invited to make is the first of its kind ever undertaken. A man holding the holy Apostleship, a "special witness" for Christ, is going in the authority of his calling to visit fields heretofore unvisited by any such authority: Tahiti, Samoa, Tonga, New Zealand, Australia, and India.

Seemingly the party will have an attentive and all-powerful advance agent, so that no concern need be felt regarding accommodations. The steamship company may tell you their lists are already filled and no more passengers can be accepted. Pay no attention to them, for your agent has a way of securing just what you need at the last moment and in the face of difficulties which apparently are insurmountable. One inclined toward skepticism may say this agent's name is Chance; but among those who believe in the authority which sent the party out and in the promises which were made, there will be no disposition to give chance the credit for the remarkable things which transpired. You will become acquainted with the leader of the expedition. Perhaps many will say, "We already know him," but accompany us and you will later confess that you knew him merely by sight. Upon returning you will really know him—not a mere bowing acquaintance, but actually having become the friend of his bosom.

And thereby a study in psychology will be presented, the like of which cannot be found elsewhere. The man who leads you believes, even claims he knows, he is a personal representative of Christ the

Lord. He feels keenly his authority, the dignity and greatness of his appointment which would not be exchanged for the wealth of kingdoms. It will be interesting to note how the high calling affects the individual and how you will react toward the Apostle and toward the man after a year of almost hourly association.

People on their knees will kiss his hand, bathing it meanwhile with sincere tears, and he will graciously submit; others likewise will be seen kissing the hands of other church potentates. These two experiences may awaken widely divergent impulses in your heart. The thoughtful observer will demand of himself adequate reasons for the difference, and these may perhaps be found.

Of course it is understood that you are not to go in person. In The Church of Jesus Christ of Latter-day Saints, men are called and set apart, instructed and given authority to do certain things, and "no man taketh this honour unto himself" (Hebrews 5:4). Therefore no duty is to be assigned you, and you will not only be an "uncommercial traveler," but an invisible and silent one as well.

How changed are world conditions since Joseph Smith's memorable prayer! Then, this trip would have aroused universal comment. Inventions which have brought nations so close together, steamships, steam and electric railways, telegraph and telephone, flying machines, and radio were either wholly unknown or in their infancy.

Did the effulgent light which accompanied Father and Son to this earth spread beyond the sacred grove in New York and inspire man to turn nature's laws to practical use? Present day knowledge has not only stimulated desire to travel, but modern inventions have provided ways of gratifying that desire. The time had come to preach the Gospel in all the world, and necessity demanded improved means of communication.

While still the junior member of the Quorum, President Heber J. Grant urged that one of the Twelve be sent to the South Sea Islands to visit missionaries and Church members and stabilize their spiritual values. But, notwithstanding its acknowledged merit, the idea seemed impossible of accomplishment, and no step was taken in this direction until two years after the leadership of the Church fell upon him who had first suggested it.

At a meeting of the Presidency and Apostles held October 14, 1920, Elder David O. McKay was formally called to visit the missions of the Pacific and probably to go around the world. The following day Hugh J. Cannon was asked to accompany him.

No pen can portray the joy of isolated Church members upon learning that a visit from one of the Twelve might be anticipated. Should a prophet in one of our communities today announce that Peter, senior Apostle of our Lord, would appear in person on the following Sunday and address and greet the people, their anticipation could not exceed that of Latter-day Saints residing in remote missions upon learning of Brother McKay's appointment. Keeping that thought in mind one can to an extent imagine the receptions accorded him.

His selection was a happy one. He was admirably suited for the important work, and it may be stated at the outset that he measured up to every expectation. His striking personality and genial disposition captivated Church members, and even among strangers won numberless friends for him and, even of greater importance, for the cause he represented. Even while preparations for the trip were in progress, it was discovered that his personality is built largely upon the fact that he is so tremendously and righteously human. Anything other than perfect frankness is abhorrent to his honest soul, and fellow travelers soon learned that he was a "Mormon." Sometimes the news was imparted rather abruptly as in the following instance:

It was a beautiful autumn evening in April (the reader will note this was in the Antipodes where the seasons are reversed) when the special missionaries embarked on the *Tofua* at Auckland, New Zealand, for Samoa. The best available accommodations were in a cabin with two other gentlemen. Brother Cannon retired early and did not see the unknown roommates that night. Next morning while standing before the glass, shaving, he noticed that Brother McKay and the strangers were awake. Suddenly Brother McKay said,

"The company must think highly of this cabin to put into it two ministers and two 'Mormon' missionaries."

The look of horrified astonishment on the strangers' faces, as revealed by the mirror, was almost more than the man before the glass could endure without an explosion. There was a long and, except for the humor of it, painful silence. The ministers had nothing to say, and Brother McKay evidently felt nothing more was necessary at that time. One of these men was seasick during the entire voyage to Fiji, where he disembarked. With the other, the missionaries subsequently became excellent friends and had many interesting interviews.

Another incident illustrative of Brother McKay's character may be related here. He and his companions, including the late Joseph Wilford Booth, had traveled from Beirut on the Mediterranean to Baalbeck, "city of the sun," in Syria, a journey over the famed mountains of Lebanon, to which detailed reference will be made in proper order. Darkness was upon them before Baalbeck was reached, and as they were to take train next morning for Aleppo, their only opportunity to see the noted ruins of the Temple of Baal was to do so as day was breaking. A guide proffered to show the place for a trifling sum and a bargain was made.

To gain access to the grounds, on the following morning, the visitors were obliged to go through a deep, dry moat, then climb over the gate. This fact and something said later at the hotel prompted Brother McKay to make enquiries, from which he learned that visitors to these ruins are expected to pay for admission. Though his train was due to leave shortly, he hastily dispatched a messenger with the entrance fees, and the gratified keeper of the grounds ran breathlessly to the station just in time to thank Brother McKay, who was well known at least to the hotel people as a "Mormon," for his honesty.

To increase the numberless accounts of world trips, viewed from one standpoint, is quite inexcusable. But because of its nature this tour made history for the Church, and it seems proper that the important incidents be recorded. Then, too, it was so filled with faith-promoting experiences, the nearness of the Almighty was so unmistakably evident, that to preserve an account of it in book form seems justifiable.

The task of preparing the work is a formidable one, but if an account sufficiently graphic could be prepared to make the reader, even in a slight degree, participate with the travelers in experiences had in China, in Hawaii, the Holy Land, indeed in every country they visited, the time devoted to its preparation would be well spent. Attention has been given to a natural human tendency to indulge in exaggeration as the incidents fall into perspective. Occurrences of minor importance are often made to appear epochal. A sincere effort to guard against such danger has been made, by constant reference to the two daily journals kept during the trip.

There is one consoling thought connected with this effort: Being a description of a journey around the world it should be easy to keep on the subject.

It may not be amiss to state thus early in the narrative that reference to a duty satisfactorily accomplished by the author is made with no boastful spirit. The reader may recall the experience of Philemon O. Merrill when the Prophet Joseph commanded him to throw an offensive braggart in a wrestling bout. He suddenly became endowed with superhuman strength and easily succeeded in a task ordinarily quite beyond his power. So it was when Brother McKay asked the writer to do certain things; in no single instance were they impossible, notwithstanding they often appeared so, but on the contrary were usually accomplished with singular ease.

In this Church frequent reference is made to Nephi's statement "The Lord giveth no commandments unto the children of men, save he shall prepare a way for them that they may accomplish the thing which he commandeth them" (1 Nephi 3:7). Another truth is that the Lord also prepares the way for his people to obey ordinary instructions given by Church leaders. Perhaps this deserves a word of amplification. One can understand the natural reluctance of the authorities to say, "Do as we advise and you will be blessed," but a century of Church history proves that the safe course is to follow counsel. "And the day cometh that they who will not hear the voice of the Lord, neither the voice of his servants, neither give heed to the words of the prophets and apostles, shall be cut off from among the people" (D&C 1:14). Whether the instruction is to secure accommodations on a crowded steamship, or to plant certain crops, to build canals, or fill foreign missions, the faithful Latter-day Saint feels he can do not only the thing which the Lord commands, but also that which is simply asked of him by those who are sustained as prophets, seers, and revelators.

Waterfall, Hawaii

Japanese Bridge

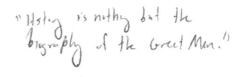

"History is nothing but the biography of the Great Men."

CHAPTER 2

EN ROUTE TO JAPAN

"The courage we desire and prize is not the courage to die decently but to live manfully."

(honorably)

—Thomas Carlyle

1795 – 1881
Scottish historian

In the Salt Lake Temple, on December 2, 1920, the special missionaries were set apart for their work by the Presidency and the Twelve. This occasion merits attention because of the inspired promises which were made and their subsequent miraculous fulfillment. Had the travelers expressed the innermost desires of their hearts, the result could hardly have been more satisfactory. No prophet of old ever spoke with more certainty than did President Grant, as he pronounced a blessing upon Brother McKay, stating among other things that he should have power to avoid dangers both seen and unseen and that his course should be directed by the whisperings of the divine spirit.

To men going into strange lands, meeting tempests, tropical heat, possibly wrecks on vessels or trains, or contagious diseases, what more desirable promise could be made?

The late President Anthon H. Lund was called to lead in blessing Brother Cannon. Some apprehension had been felt as to what might happen, such as inconvenient delays, should serious sickness overtake either one of the party. Brother Cannon was particularly concerned, for shortly before, he had suffered from a painful illness. But anxiety vanished with the words: "We bless you that you may have <u>health</u> <u>and strength on your journey,</u> that sickness may have no power over you; but if seasickness or anything like that comes, it will be of short duration."

Attentive readers will see how literally these promises were fulfilled. Little did the travelers think then that never again, in mortal life, would they hear the voice of that kindly saint, President Anthon H. Lund, the man whom everybody loved.

Missionary work has developed courage of a high and unusual order. And this quality in its perfection is not shown by the men who go. They are crusaders, so to speak, marching to martial music, and inspired also at the thought of the new experiences which await them. But the valorous wives who remain behind have no such stimulant. They face a colorless and difficult period, with loneliness playing the chief role. Saying good-bye is never easy. In this instance it was doubly hard because shortly before, Sister McKay had presented her husband with a sturdy son and Sister Cannon had given to hers a beautiful daughter, and neither of these good women had fully regained her strength.

On December 4, 1920, the train was boarded for Portland. Pleasant and profitable was the two hour interview, as the travelers neared Pocatello, with Elder Fred A. Cain, now president of the Idaho Falls Stake, who for eight years was a missionary among the Nipponese. This observant man gave information about Japan, the first objective after leaving America, which was very helpful.

To lovers of scenic beauty, the ride from Utah to Oregon is a delightful one. For many miles the pine-clad hills were covered with snow, blending white with green into a beautiful picture.

A brief stay in Portland—three and a half hours—permitted the missionaries to attend Sunday evening service in a Church-owned chapel, which would be a credit to any ward in Utah. They met a number of friends, made new acquaintances, were entertained in the mission home by President Heber C. Iverson and his good wife and family, and had a short drive about the city.

The stopover in Seattle was of even shorter duration: one and a half hours, but long enough to have a little visit with Elders Reed Michelsen and William S. Maxwell who, on a raw winter morning long before daylight, were awaiting the belated train.

A conference had just been held in Bellingham and the missionaries in attendance were at the station to wish the brethren a pleasant journey as the train passed through.

The depression incident to leaving the land of the Stars and Stripes was somewhat allayed in Vancouver by the hearty welcome received from missionaries and others. Brother Stephen Markham Dudley, grandson of that loyal man, Stephen Markham, who was often with the Prophet in the troublous days of Nauvoo, and by whose side Brother Joseph slept in Carthage the night prior to his martyrdom, placed himself and his auto at the disposal of the visitors, and after visas for passports and arrangements for transportation were completed a question arose in their minds as to how this could have been accomplished without his aid. His jolly little wife, eager to visit with one of the general Church authorities, not only rode with the party, but to their wonderment found time to prepare an excellent dinner for fifteen people.

The predominant thought after meeting the missionaries in and about Vancouver, and indeed in every field, is one of surprise that they are so misunderstood. More than a score of them were present, several lady missionaries among the number, all conscientiously devoting their time, meanwhile paying their own expenses, to broadcast the message of "Mormonism." Let us pause to look into their faces, indicative of lofty ideals. One sees no fanaticism, only a sublime and cheerful confidence; no egotism, only trustfulness in the Almighty; no smugness, only humility. Had a prophet arisen and foretold that all were destined to die as martyrs, hardly a cheek would have blanched. But had he declared that one among them would lose his most priceless possession, virtue, it would have caused most poignant grief. They were ready, to the last man, to die for the Gospel, and were also determined to do the more heroic thing: live for it.

This tour took the travelers into fifteen mission fields and brought them into close contact with fully three hundred missionaries. What is said of Church representatives in Vancouver is true of all; not that the missionaries are precisely what the Church would have them. Many are inexperienced and a few are ignorant, some inexcusably and embarrassingly so, but with surprisingly few exceptions their personal lives are above reproach. Furthermore, they are almost always dignified ladies and gentlemen, a credit to the cause they represent.

The statement regarding the moral character of missionaries is received with surprise or incredulity by strangers. When they learn that young men, often of tender years, are sent from farm or shop or school to face the temptations met in great cities, they are more than ever disinclined to believe the statement, and if partially convinced, they ask whence comes the power which enables those boys to remain clean.

What is the answer? It cannot be given in a sentence. First, they are called, ordained, and assigned to their fields by men who are themselves strictly virtuous. A statement attributed to Confucius illustrates the importance of this point. The noted philosopher held a position of trust in one of the Chinese provinces, and all associated with him were renowned for their impeccable honesty. A neighboring ruler, whose district had exactly the opposite reputation, called on Confucius and asked, "What can I do to end the vicious dishonesty which exists in my department?"

"Return home and be honest yourself," was Confucius's simple answer.

In their homes these missionaries are taught that it is better to lose life than virtue. The Book of Mormon tells them that sexual sin, murder excepted, is the most grievous in the eyes of the Almighty. At the meeting of missionaries in Vancouver, one Elder read from the Doctrine and Covenants: "Let virtue garnish thy thoughts unceasingly; then shall thy confidence wax strong in the presence of God. . . . The Holy Ghost shall be thy constant companion" (D&C 121:45-46).

The writer of this account recalls two solemn occasions to

which he was an unhappy witness. One, missionaries, almost broken-hearted, were called together to excommunicate from the Church an associate who had forgotten his covenants and fallen into transgression. Bitter tears were shed by the accused and by those sitting in judgment on the case.

The other occasion was when a white-haired father and his family surrounded the casket in which a son had been brought home from the mission field. With tears streaming down his cheeks and with broken voice the father spoke: "Our boy has come home, has returned to us in a coffin, but thank God he has come home clean."

This, perhaps, answers the strangers' questions. It is the great vitalizing power with the missionaries which keeps their moral fiber from decay.

Thus far the trip was filled with delightful incidents, every moment pleasantly spent, but evidently it was to be a working not a pleasure trip, for diligence is one of Brother McKay's outstanding characteristics.

Yokohama, principal seaport of Japan, lies almost directly west of San Francisco. Our younger readers, and perhaps some older ones, may wonder why the nearest way to Yokohama is to travel north until the snowy mountains of the Aleutian Islands are visible. This is due to the fact that the earth, being nearly round, is more narrow as one goes north.

Numerous invitations to dinners and other social affairs where refreshments were served were extended to the special missionaries during the weeks immediately preceding their departure. Such acts, intended as kindness and greatly appreciated, were poor preparation for a rough ocean voyage. Some of these delightful dinners were destined to come up later in a most distressing manner.

Have you ever been aboard a vessel on an extremely rough sea? Have you felt it roll and toss and plunge, then when struck full force by a mighty wave which washes its decks, felt it shudder and tremble as though it had received a death blow and must assuredly sink? And all the while the stomachs of the sensitive passengers are performing similar evolutions and are dancing about as wildly as the ship itself.

Frequently not more than a dozen people out of several hundred passengers were at meals.

Here was seen the first evidence of the prophetic power of those who set the special missionaries apart. Brother Cannon had never been a good sailor. On previous journeys he had invariably been seasick if the water was rough, but here the words of President Lund were literally fulfilled. Brother McKay, being the leader of this tour, maintained his supremacy in the matter of seasickness as in all other things. He does nothing by halves, but treats every subject exhaustively, going to the very bottom of it, and this occasion was no exception. Seasickness is undertaken with the same vigorous energy which he displays in running for a train. In either case those in front should dodge.

The following excerpts from a letter, written by him to friends at home, will prove interesting:

"You remember what Oliver Wendell Holmes says about an 'outer' door and an 'inner' door to every person's feelings? Well, since you are dear friends to whom the inner door of my feelings has always been open, I think I will give you some of my inside history of this never-to-be-forgotten voyage.

"Brother Hugh J. and I were in prime condition, I thought, when we boarded the *Empress of Japan* on the evening of December 7, 1920. Kind friends had showered us with good wishes and blessings, had feted and dined us for weeks previous, and had sent along with us boxes of the choicest cream chocolates to make our journey sweet and delightsome. Even as we walked up the gangplank at Vancouver, we were accompanied by a score of Elders and Saints, who, with President Iverson, bade us a heartfelt Bon Voyage.

"It was storming when we left port, and the movement of the boat was keenly perceptible even before we went to sleep. The pitching of the vessel in the night awoke me and every nerve and muscle of my body responded to the movement of the boat. As this movement became more pronounced and intense, the contents of my digestive organs joined in unison with nerves and muscles. Twenty-one years ago, one morning on the Atlantic, I had experienced a similar feeling, so I knew I had better dress carefully and get on deck. At that moment Brother Cannon jumped out of bed as bright and pert as a ten-year-old boy. He would steady himself as though he were anchored. With no apparent difficulty he dressed himself and even shaved: an operation, which, though ordinarily simple enough, seemed to me under the circumstances, almost marvelous. I concluded to take his advice, when he said: 'If you aren't feeling well, I suggest you don't look in the mirror.'

"No, I wouldn't eat breakfast, probably would feel better if I fasted. It was a dismal sounding gong that called us to breakfast, anyhow: a fitting accompaniment to the gloom of the weather. However, before attempting to dress I ate an apple which Hugh J. handed me. Without hurry I put on my clothes and started for the deck; but the swaying staircase and the madly moving world of water stirred my feelings with a desire for solitude. Yielding, I hurried to my room, where in less time than it takes to tell you, the apple and I parted company forever. I wondered what there was in common between a Jonathan apple and a Jonah that would produce such like effects. Though I arrived at no definite conclusion, one thing was most certain: My sympathy was wholly with the whale. I understood, too, how Jonah escaped being thrown into the sea. If I could have entirely followed the whale's example, I, too, would have swum for land.

"Hugh J. returned from breakfast looking as robust and rosy as an athlete. . . . Limp and dejected, I looked at him, healthy and happy, and began, right then and there, to doubt the wisdom of the Revolutionary statesman who declared that 'all men are created equal.'

"Feeling somewhat better, I started again for the deck, and was not a little consoled when I passed a poor Chinaman with perspiration standing in beads on his jaundiced-looking face, and sitting holding his knees looking, as I'm sure he felt, the most forsaken, limpy lump of humanity in existence.

"At any rate, I had company in furnishing amusement for the chosen few. This time I reached only the top of the stairs when that intense yearning to be alone drove me back to my cabin. Good-bye last night's dinner! Good-bye yesterday's luncheon! And during the next sixty hours, good-bye everything I had ever eaten since I was a babe on Mother's knee! I'm not sure I didn't cross the threshold into the pre-existent state.

"In the tossing and heaving of the ship, as well as of internal conditions, there was no respite. She would mount the crest of a huge wave then plunge head-on; but before hitting the bottom of the trough, she would plunge to 'port,' then instantly veer to 'starboard;' hesitating a moment, she would shiver and plunge again: turning, veering, 'shimmying,' in endless repetition until it seemed that life was made up of nothing else. The dance floor is not the only place where disgraceful, degenerate movements may lead to ill.

"And all this was on the placid Pacific! Heaven be merciful to me if we sail a tempestuous sea.

"Thursday I managed to eat a little soup and retain it. Friday, though the sea began heaving with renewed vigor, I continued to gain. One incident that day proved a very great impetus to my speedy convalescence. Brother Hugh hadn't been quite so brisk as usual, and I noticed that his rosy cheek had a somewhat faded hue; but he went to breakfast as usual, thus maintaining his excellent record of not having missed a meal. I was still holding pretty close to the old berth. About 10:30 he came in somewhat flushed about the face but pale about the mouth and eyes. For a moment, neither of us said anything; then the humor of the situation getting the mastery, he said, 'I guess I might as well confess to you that I've just had my turn.' In the interim of laughter, he explained that after breakfast he went to the library to write some letters, when all at once he became aware of an unpleasant feeling creeping over him. With the instinct of his sea-faring ancestors, he started for the pure sea breezes that were blowing on deck; but suddenly the company of fellow passengers became most objectionable and turning his back upon them, he started downstairs most unceremoniously.

Fortunately, he managed to reach the passageway leading to our room, when, Presto! He reached seclusion, but the deck behind him looked like the 'milky way.' The incomprehensible thing to me is that this spontaneous outburst ended his seasickness.

"We had a pretty rough voyage, and a cold one, having sailed so far north that we could glimpse the snow-capped mountains of the Aleutian Islands. However, messages received disclose the fact that the *Monteagle*, a sister ship to ours, though she left eight days before we did is only a comparatively short distance ahead of us with most of her lifeboats washed overboard. Undoubtedly, she was in the center of the sweeping gale."

The *Empress of Japan*, the Ship Carrying the
Missionaries from Vancouver to Yokohama

CHAPTER 3

LAND OF ASTONISHING SIGHTS AND EXPERIENCES

"He drew a circle that shut me out:
Heretic, rebel, a thing to flout.
But love and I had the wit to win!
We drew a circle that took him in."

—Edwin Markham
1852–1940
American Poet

A mortal! His life like a torrential mountain stream dashing against jagged rocks, foaming, roaring, then finding quiet places of depth and restfulness, places of meditation and with opportunity to pray that it may not dissipate itself in purposeless spray! What a study he is for his fellowmen. This is particularly true aboard ship where one has time for contemplation. What secrets, hopes, and ambitions are locked in the breast of the gentleman sitting opposite? On deck a woman makes a heroic effort to smile, but one suspects her heart is leaden, for there was something akin to tragedy on her face as the vessel left port. It would make a pungent picture if the story of these lives were thrown upon a screen. And how startling it would be if such a picture were embellished by the thoughts of the actors! There would be pathos and comedy, tragedy, despair, and

19

romance, with all their variations.

Here is unmistakable culture making the society of this passenger very delightful, but unfortunately others are of quite a different class. However, the observant person learns that it is unwise arbitrarily to classify fellow travelers. Not infrequently some, at first highly rated, prove disappointing in one particular or another; and often those looked upon with less favor show admirable qualities.

A case in point was a lady aboard the *Empress of Japan*, who was traveling with her husband. A handsome, though rather coarse-appearing and loud-speaking woman, her conduct was offensive to many of the passengers. But the maternal tenderness she exhibited toward the children of a lady who was ill touched the hearts of all who saw it. As she cuddled one curly little head into her breast, tears came into her eyes; her hoydenish spirit was subdued and chastened, another instance of a helpless child calling forth the angelic instincts of true womanhood. A man who had often been heard to flatter her, remarked that she was a beautiful flower. She retorted, "A flower! Bah! I'm nothing but a weed." Then as she pressed the little head closer to her bosom, she wistfully added, "But I'm a better weed for having held this little one in my arms."

Crossing the 180th meridian, that mythical line running from the north to the south pole is a time of interest aboard ship. The west bound traveler who crosses this line loses a day, when east bound he gains one. For instance, our travelers retired Tuesday night, December 14th, and arose the following morning on Thursday, the 16th. Had they been sailing eastward and reached this line Tuesday evening, they would have retired as usual, and next morning it would still be Tuesday. This arrangement was made by mutual consent of all civilized nations, and the 180th meridian was chosen because it traverses the Pacific Ocean, touching practically none of the islands, and consequently this arbitrary change of days does not disrupt social, religious, or business affairs.

The necessity for such an adjustment is obvious. Suppose the reader enters upon a trip around the world. Going west, he of course travels with the sun and is obliged daily to turn his watch back to keep the correct time. Upon returning to the starting point he would have turned his watch back twenty-four hours, thereby losing an entire day. He would think it was Saturday when in reality it would be Sunday. Conversely, when encircling the globe traveling east, the watch is set forward each day. Of course the days are shorter than normal, and upon returning the traveler has gained twenty-four hours. He would think it was Sunday when it was Saturday. The change made at the 180th meridian equalizes this difference, whatever the direction of one's travels, and keeps the days of the week straight for the whole world.

Incidentally it furnishes our missionaries with an unanswerable argument against those who, notwithstanding the importance they attach to their day of worship, are still influenced by an imaginary and man-made line. It is an actual fact that people living in the South Sea Islands, and but a few miles apart, worship on different days.

During the night of December 22nd, the missionaries emerged from an extremely gloomy and tempestuous winter into what seemed a balmy spring. What a difference sunshine makes in our lives! Nature had changed moods and even morose passengers followed her example.

The *Empress* was anchored just outside the breakwater of Yokohama harbor. Rosy tints of the rising sun spread over serene sea and landscape, and a fleet of white-sailed smacks making for their fishing fields added brilliancy to the scene. Off in the distance the sacred mountain of Japan, Fujiyama, majestic in its covering of snow but its natural austerity lessened by the mellow morning light, presented an inspiring picture. The justly famous "glow" of early morning in the Swiss Alps, about which one often reads and too seldom sees, was visible in all its glory on Fujiyama, though it was one hundred miles away.

Imagine, if you can, being aboard a great airplane which had conveyed you to some distant inhabited planet. Think what your feelings would be as the craft settled gently to its landing place and you looked eagerly over the vessel's side at the expectant groups awaiting your arrival. Your emotions, as you viewed their strange features and attire and listened to their incomprehensible chatter, would probably not be greatly unlike those of the traveler just emerging from well known Occidental scenes to the unfamiliar ones of the Orient. Here, too, one enters a new world. The people, themselves so different in features and dress from the Europeans, the buildings, temples, pagodas, and shrines, rickshas drawn by fleet-footed youths, heavy wagons drawn by men or oxen or small horses or by a combination of all three, all were as unusual as if the stranger were indeed arriving on a heretofore unknown planet.

But no! After running the gauntlet of custom officials he attempts to cross the street and is in grave danger of colliding with an intimate acquaintance—one might say a rattling good friend—a Ford automobile. One feels inclined to pick it up and hug it, such is the delight at seeing something so familiar.

Without counting small isles whose coastline is less than two and a half miles, Japan is composed of nearly five hundred islands, 162 square miles, approximately but twice the size of Utah. When it is remembered that but one twelfth of the land is arable and that it supports approximately sixty million people, one can understand the phenomenal economy which is a potent cause of the country's greatness. Every child has thought of the Chinese and Japanese as standing with their feet up and heads hanging down. We adults view their habits in a similar light. It is a land of incongruities. On every hand, the European meets with, to him, highly interesting and even astonishing sights and experiences. In passing, it might be noted that in Japan all who are not Oriental are European. The ladies have their hair dressed in a quaint but artistic fashion and, even on the streets, wear kimonos whose color and design might well arouse the envy of their foreign sisters; but the clumsy wooden sandals detract much from their appearance. A few Japanese maidens, shod thus, tripping daintily along the paved streets make almost as much noise as a band of wild horses would do.

During most of the year the profusion of flowers gives off a delicate perfume, but with this are mingled many offensive odors. One is delayed on the street by a cumbersome oxcart or must wait while a swarm of rickshas flit by, and sees flying overhead a strictly modern airplane. The people remove their shoes, or the strips of wood which answer therefore, upon entering a house or church, or even a store, but hats need not necessarily be removed. They eat with chopsticks which are hardly as thick as, though slightly longer than a lead pencil, and the dexterity displayed in taking two of these sticks in one hand and with them picking up all kinds of food is indeed surprising.

The Japanese are said to bathe oftener than any other people in the world, and no home is complete without a bathroom. Often these are exposed to the weather and gaze of the curious passerby in summertime and are only partially protected from wintry blasts by bamboo screens which can be raised or lowered at will. President Grant, who was the first missionary from our Church to Japan and who is well acquainted with Nipponese customs, says when one has visitors in that land it is regarded as a compliment to ask them to bathe.

For generations these people have had the habit of sitting on their feet, not cross-legged as the Pacific Islanders do, but with the feet bent back under them. They tire when they sit on chairs; and in trains and even in the meetings which were held, they often climbed on benches or chairs and doubled their feet under them. Some writers attribute the universal shortness of Japanese legs to this habit.

Babies are carried on their mother's backs, as the American Indians do, and women frequently engage in very hard labor while thus burdened. And speaking of babies, one is reminded of the curious Japanese method of reckoning age. A child born December 31st is considered two years old on January 1st, because it has lived in two different years.

In most countries the purchaser who buys in quantities obtains a better price, but the reverse is true in Japan. For example, Brother McKay wanted a pencil, the price of which was two sen. It was learned that twelve would cost twenty-five sen. A single collar cost fifty sen; half a dozen would cost seventy sen each. The underlying thought is based on justice. A person wealthy enough to buy in quantities should pay a higher price. For this reason they have a price for the man who walks to the store, a higher one for him who rides in a ricksha; and he who rides in an auto must pay the maximum.

The politeness of the Japanese is proverbial. A stranger could not easily lose himself. He enquires the way to a certain place. Perhaps the person addressed does not understand him, but usually he will stop every passerby until one is found who does understand, and will often accompany the stranger and point out the way or even go with him to his destination. The man or woman whose hair is beginning to turn gray is never permitted to stand in a street car, and the conductors on cars and trains lift their caps and ask for fares or tickets most apologetically.

The story is told of two travelers who enquired the way to a certain street. The man accosted did not possess the desired information and stood in embarrassment while they walked on. A moment later they heard him calling and waited while he ran breathlessly to them. He fairly exuded apologies: "Will you kindly pardon my inexcusable ignorance in not being able to give you the information you asked for? My brother came along, just after you left me, and I asked him, and to my shame he did not know either."

Trained as he is in Sunday School procedure and loving the work as he does, one cannot imagine Brother McKay being embarrassed by a crowd of Sunday School children; and still he was visibly so at the first School he attended in Tokyo. A number of children came to the Mission House. Except for the fact that the boys wore plain kimonos and the girls gaily colored ones, there was little difference in their dress. Brother McKay wanted to greet them properly and held out his hand for that purpose, but their surprised glances traveled from his hand to his face, to ascertain if possible what they were expected to do. Later he learned that shaking hands is an unknown custom with them. One might go on almost indefinitely describing Japanese peculiarities, but time and space forbid. Suffice it to say that they are an extremely courteous and delightfully interesting people and one sails regretfully away from their land.

The Gospel has not made great headway in Japan. Comparatively few hearts have been touched by the divine power. The people through curiosity will investigate, but they do so as they might study a scientific theory, and while recognizing its worth as a splendid moral and social system, they fail to discover its divinity. One could not find a better exemplification of the statement that the things of God cannot be understood except through his spirit. The devotion of the few into whose hearts the convincing testimony had really entered, resembled that of faithful Church members the world over. But some have accepted the Gospel merely as an experiment and in much the same spirit which they manifest in adopting European clothing that can be laid aside at will.

Elder David O. McKay and President Hugh J.
Cannon with Rickshas in the Background

Hotel in Yokahama, Japan

CHAPTER 4

THE JAPANESE MISSION

"The first and best victory is to conquer self; to be conquered by self is, of all things, the most shameful and vile."

—Plato

[handwritten: ↦ Control over the Natural Man]

The Japanese Mission at the time of the visit herein described was in charge of President Joseph H. Stimpson, then nearing the end of his second term of service there, having spent a total of eleven years in that field. His wife accompanied him as a bride on the last mission and at the time of this visit they had three beautiful children, the oldest of which talked Japanese as fluently as he did English. Perhaps no better opportunity will present itself to say that Sister Stimpson is one of the gems of the Church, hospitable, industrious, and willing to expatriate herself because of her deep and abiding love for missionary work.

The Mission Home was a comfortable one. Conforming to usual Japanese custom, the visitors were immediately invited to bathe, and having heard of the novel methods, they were glad to accept. A fire is built in the iron box in one end of the tub, which in this instance was a wooden affair about four feet deep and nearly as wide. This oven heats the water almost to the boiling point. The bather is supposed

27

to wash himself thoroughly, for which purpose there is a basin, soap, and hose with running water; then he climbs into the tub and soaks in water as hot as it is humanly possible to have it and live. Thus the entire family bathes in the same water without having it become very dirty.

Even in so-called heathen Japan, elaborate decorations were made in honor of the Christmas holidays. On each side of the door in front of many buildings, a bunch of pine branches and bamboo canes were to be seen. It is said the pine indicates a desire for long life, and the bamboo expresses other good wishes. Under President Stimpson's direction an interesting Christmas program was given at the home. The natives sat on mats on the floor with feet doubled up under them for nearly three hours and apparently enjoyed it.

Meetings were attended by the special missionaries in Tokyo, Kofu, and Osaka. The people listen attentively, but it is rather discouraging to think that after almost twenty years of earnest work there were but 125 Church members in Japan. Brother McKay intended going to Hokkaido on the north island where there was a branch of the Church. A start was made with Brother and Sister Stimpson and their baby in the party.

The steamer, plying between the islands, was anchored in the open sea and a tug conveyed the passengers to it. A violent storm was raging, and even before the tug left its pier it began bucking after the fashion of a western bronco. Passengers resembled animated shuttlecocks. Sister Stimpson literally tossed her baby to Brother Cannon while she threw sundry other things to the fishes. This was her first experience with the malady. As the tug came alongside the steamer, the danger of attempting to jump from one vessel to the other became evident. One moment they would crash violently together and the next would be so far apart that even a trained broad jumper could not make the spring. A strong impression to turn back came to Brother McKay, and though greatly disappointed all agreed it would be unwise to proceed in the face of this feeling.

The suitcases, etc., were being shifted to the steamer when President Stimpson's attention was called to the fact that he was losing his luggage.

He turned, and his face, a pitiful mixture of ashy gray and yellowish green, confirmed his words: "My luggage isn't the only thing I'm losing."

It should be recorded to Brother McKay's credit that in this case he escaped seasickness by an extremely narrow margin.

It will never be known what would have occurred had they gone on, but having in mind the prophetic words that the head of this tour should be inspired to avoid dangers seen and unseen, no one would have dared disregard the impression.

The Japanese are as modest as the Yankees, and not a whit more so, when talking of their own land. One is not justified in speaking of the beautiful, they say, until Nikko has been seen. It is truly a delightful place and a visit there vindicates in large measure the pride which the natives have in it. The ornate temples and "sacred" places are bewildering in number and beauty, though some of the beauty borders on the grotesque. Indeed, throughout Japan there is a mixture of the sublime and what to the European is the ridiculous, how sublime and ridiculous only those know who have visited the land.

At all "sacred" places the visitors had to remove their shoes, and at the "Sanctum Sanctorum" they were obliged to discard overcoats as well, despite extremely cold weather.

President Stimpson tells of three Elders who visited this place and were told at the door that no one without faith could enter.

"We have faith," was the missionary's reply.

"If you have faith, you may come in for one yen each."

"But we have more faith than that," replied the Elder. "We have faith that we can all come in for one yen." Their faith was effective.

One's stock of adjectives is exhausted in attempting to describe the carvings and decorations on the buildings. Here are the originals of the three monkeys, one of which holds his hand over eyes, one over mouth and one over ears, indicating that man should see no evil, speak no evil, and hear no evil. The cryptomeria trees are as indescribable as the temples. They are extremely tall and stately evergreens, many of them six or seven feet in diameter and some of them much more than that.

At one place many stone lanterns about six feet high were seen, and among them was one which, according to tradition, had formed the intolerable habit of turning into a ghost and frightening everybody away, so a wire cage was placed around it. Since then it has behaved properly.

After viewing the river, the waterfalls, forests, temples, and shrines one leaves the place with the feeling that the Japanese are not far wrong in their boastful statement regarding its beauty.

In the car with Brother McKay and his party between Nikko and Tokyo were a number of natives. In one corner was a dainty young lady attired in the usual attractive Japanese style, with elaborate hair dressing, highly colored and beautiful kimono, stockings which reached to her ankles, and the inevitable wooden sandals. She was accompanied by a young man and an older lady, and in due time they opened a package of lunch. Chopsticks, kept in sealed wax paper as a sanitary measure, were used to pick up the food, not a particle of which was touched by the hands. The skill displayed in using these sticks attracted the attention of our curious Americans and perhaps they watched the diners more intently than good breeding would permit. The lunch reminded them that thoughtful Sister Stimpson had brought along a box of sandwiches and they too began their meal.

Think how an American eats a sandwich! He takes it in one hand, or perhaps in two, and tears away at it very much as a bear would do. It was not long until, instead of being observers, the Americans became the observed. A little girl sitting opposite tried vainly not to smile. Too polite to laugh openly, she turned her head and looked out of the window to conceal her amusement.

The missionaries believed their hands were clean at the commencement of the meal, but at its conclusion Brother McKay went to the washroom and, when he rejoined his party, remarked, "Do you know what those people said as I came by them? If they did not actually say it they thought, 'Now that he has eaten with his dirty hands he has washed them.'"

After all, many habits which seem peculiar or even ridiculous to us might be imitated with profit.

On a part of this trip, it was not possible to secure accommodations in anything but the first class sleeper, and in the mission field to travel first class is not usually deemed compatible with the proper spirit of humility. Brother McKay, however, consoled his associates by telling of Brother Fjelsted's prayer, "Give us de best dere is, Lord, for you know, Lord, de best is none too good for us."

Some of our readers will remember Brother Fjelsted as a good old Danish brother, now gone to a splendid reward, who was one of the First Council of Seventy.

Having letters of introduction to Dr. Kamada, president of the Kaio University at Tokyo, and Mr. Konoto, immigration commissioner of Japan, Brother McKay and his party called on them. Both of these gentlemen had been in America and spoke English fluently. The university president was surrounded by professors and other guests who were eating, drinking, and smoking in his office. The other gentleman was visited at his home. When the maid opened the door at the last named place, she dropped on her knees and bowed until her head touched the floor. Visitors must remove their shoes before entering a Japanese home and as the weather was cold our travelers had taken their slippers with them. This gentleman was the embodiment of courtesy and expressed a desire to aid Brother McKay or the missionaries in every way. The maid brought cups of coffee and presented them to the visitors, first dropping on her knees. When it was explained that they would prefer hot water instead of coffee, that was brought with equal courtesy. These visits were made on January 1st, there, as at home, a great holiday. Bands were out in gorgeous uniforms. Gaily dressed men, women, and children thronged the streets, and the colors were remarkable and in some cases startling. Street cars were crowded; almost every ricksha was in use, a large number of them having two men, tandem fashion, so that greater speed could be attained and a more elaborate display made. Many of the ricksha men were barelegged, but President

Stimpson said one must be here in the summer to see bare legs at their best—or worst.

Few experiences come to Church members which are more inspirational than to attend a missionary meeting in the field. The courage, faith, and devotion of our young men, their exemplary and self-sacrificing lives, bear a most eloquent testimony of the divinity of this work. No sermon, howsoever gifted the speaker, is comparable to this practical demonstration of desire to serve one's fellowmen.

The meeting held in Tokyo was as a rich feast to a hungry man. Elders Myrl L. Bodily and Whitaker had come in from Hokkaido, where they were laboring with energy and ability. The same spirit was manifested by Elders Owen McGary and John Hicken, laboring in Osaka, Elders Pyne and Holley from Kofu, and Elder Howard Jensen who, with President and Sister Stimpson, was working in Tokyo.

To think of these young and inexperienced missionaries and their earnest efforts to redeem a benighted people is to praise the Lord. One is reminded of other modest characters, now acknowledged heroes, the ancient prophets and apostles of the Bible and the early leaders of the Church.

If further evidence of the divinity of this work were needed, it could be found in the love which characterizes the missionary. With possibly one exception, the visitors had met none of these brethren before; but still they seemed to be lifelong acquaintances: nay, more than that, of one family, brothers in the flesh instead of merely in belief. As the visiting party boarded the train for Osaka, the Elders remaining in Tokyo ran along the platform to again press Brother McKay's hand and hear his words, "The Lord bless you, my brother."

Nara, former capital of the empire, is not far behind Nikko as a showplace. Its artistic park is full of deer, believed by the Japanese to be sacred. They will eat from a stranger's hand. There was a sacred horse, which, probably due to ignorance on the subject, looked like a common glass-eyed cayuse. There were sacred pigeons, temples, and bells. It would appear that nearly everything is sacred to a Japanese except his promise, but unless he is outrageously maligned he esteems a promise as the least sacred thing in the world.

Fourteen hours with an express train carried the travelers from Osaka to Shimonoseki, the point of embarkation for Pusan, in Korea. As they proceeded southward the climate became milder and before the sea was reached many heavily laden orange trees were seen. Men and women were plowing their rice fields, if drawing a pointed stick to which a cow is hitched, through mud almost knee deep can be called plowing.

Comfortable quarters were obtained aboard the *Komo Maru* which plies between this Japanese island and the mainland of Asia. As the vessel left the busy and lighted harbor and entered the inky blackness which prevailed outside and the brethren thought of the strange country and people to which they were going, their own ignorance of the customs and language, they thought of another journey taken by a man oppressed with serious sickness and the exalted words which he wrote:

"Lead, kindly Light, amid th' encircling gloom;
Lead thou me on!
The night is dark, and I am far from home;
Lead thou me on!
Keep thou my feet; I do not ask to see
The distant scene—one step enough for me."

[*Hymns*, no. 97.]

Elder David O. McKay and President Hugh J.
Cannon Feeding Pigeons, Nikko, Japan

Elder David
O. McKay and
President Hugh
J. Cannon, Great
Bell, Japan

Asian Family

A Snowy Day in Aomori, Japan

The Great Wall of China

CHAPTER 5

CHINA DEDICATED FOR THE GOSPEL

"And this gospel of the kingdom shall be preached in all the world for a witness unto all nations; and then shall the end come."

—Matthew 24:14

An important part of Brother McKay's special mission was to visit China and, if he felt so impressed, to dedicate that vast realm for the preaching of the Gospel. China had a well-developed civilization twenty-five centuries before Great Britain came into existence, and her age if nothing else should command respect. The thoughtful reader will appreciate some of the difficulties which our missionaries will encounter should they be called to that land, and the duty confronting this missionary party was approached with a sincere prayer for guidance to do what the Almighty desired, and nothing more.

These brethren were not the first from our Church to set foot in China. Shortly after the people arrived in Utah, Elders Hosea Stout, James Lewis, and Chapman Duncan were sent to this benighted land. It seemed, however, that the time for preaching the Gospel to the heathens had not arrived, and little was accomplished.

The transition from bright and colorful Japan, an aggressive and virile world power in the making, to somber and gloomy China, a nation of decay and senility, is less abrupt because the traveler passes en route through Korea, an intermediate country less cheerful than the one and less funereal than the other.

Landing in Pusan, Korea, the visitors felt they were in another world, and their hasty journey through that land to Mukden, Manchuria, accentuated the feeling. The bearing and dress of the people, especially their strange and varied headgear, the clusters of homes whose color and shape make a village in the distance look like a group of toadstools, all awaken a desire to tarry and become better acquainted. Nor are the sterile, rocky stretches of land and the bleak mountains without interest, though not approaching Japan in point of beauty. Roads appear to consist mainly of footpaths, and the transportation of the country seems to be carried on the backs of cows and oxen. Yonder an immense load of straw moves along the path without any visible means of locomotion, but somewhere under the mass was a patient cow. At the same time the driver, trudging along on foot, had a huge load on his own back.

Straw appears to be the country's chief building material, as from it practically all the roofs and many of the sides of the houses in the country districts are constructed.

At Mukden it was necessary to change money into Chinese, a task approached with considerable trepidation, as travelers are warned against counterfeit money with which China is flooded. Not only was the bogus article a serious menace to the uninitiated, but bills issued by supposedly reputable banks had little or no value outside of the bank's particular district.

Brother McKay undertook to attend to this business while his companion secured railroad accommodations. The latter task was completed first and Brother Cannon found his chief standing somewhat uncertainly before a stoical Chinese money changer who had a "take it or leave it" look on his face. Brother McKay justly felt that the man was robbing him, and his Scotch blood rises in instant and vigorous rebellion at such thought. At this moment an American, who was leaving China and who had been making desperate efforts to exchange Chinese money for good American dollars, came up. The money changer's face lost some of its placidity as he saw his profits vanish while the fellow countrymen carried on their own negotiations. Not only was considerable money saved in the exchange but this gentleman gave information which subsequently was of great value to the travelers.

A glance at his map will show the reader that Mukden is far to the north and naturally in midwinter is extremely cold. From here the brethren entered China proper, another new world. And a ragged, dirty, starving, benighted, and altogether forbidding world it was. On that part of the country through which they traveled practically no rain had fallen for two years, and at the stations they were besieged by beggars whose pinched features and half-clothed bodies bore pitiful evidence of intense suffering.

A stop was made at Shanhaikuan, where so much fighting has been done during the present revolution. Here the missionaries caught their first glimpse of the Great Wall of China, one of the marvels of all time. A British engineer has figured that it contains enough material to build a wall six feet high and two feet thick which would reach around the world at the equator. As the train was to remain there for a short time the missionaries started out to obtain a nearer view of the wall and perhaps a picture, when they were so beset by hordes of beggars that further progress was impossible. Though the weather was but little if any above zero, these pitiable creatures were nearly naked. It would be a compliment to call them ragged, and if some of them were not really starving they were past masters in the art of deceiving.

En route from Mukden to Peking many Japanese soldiers were seen along the railway line and in their hearts the travelers rather resented what seemed to be an unwarranted intrusion. But at one station, and much to their surprise, they saw an American flag and a group of real U.S. soldier boys. Their surprise hardly equaled that of one young chap as Brother McKay gave him a bear hug, which, however, pleased him greatly after his astonishment had subsided. Though China at that time was comparatively peaceful, foreign powers were guarding the railway lines. This reconciled the visitors somewhat to the sight of the Japanese soldiers.

Think of a city of a million inhabitants without a streetcar or omnibus line! The principal means of transportation—indeed the only means except for one's legs and an occasional auto or a small horse-drawn carriage at the time of this visit—were the innumerable rickshas. These flit rapidly and silently through crowded streets, dextrously avoiding collisions which to the traveler appear wholly unavoidable and furnish an excellent opportunity of seeing Chinese life. A facetious American has dubbed these conveyances "pullman" cars. This was Peking.

The missionaries had some little difficulty in finding a suitable hotel through the unjustifiable interference of a man who pretended to be able to understand English, but who did not really understand it or else wilfully misled them.

These brethren can never think of January 9, 1921, without a feeling of deep solemnity. As they approached the city on the previous evening they had looked in vain for a suitable spot away from the turmoil of the place where the dedicatory prayer could be offered should Brother McKay feel so impressed. Nothing but barren fields was to be seen. As the following day was Sunday it was deemed the fitting time to attend to this duty, if it were to be done at all, and Peking seemed the proper place. The hordes of insistent and repulsive beggars made anything but a favorable impression.

However, with morning came a strong impression that the land should be dedicated for this purpose. But where to find a suitable place for the fulfillment of this duty was a serious question. It was felt that such a prayer should be offered under the blue heavens and in quiet, and from what they had seen of the city no such spot existed. Naturally this duty might have been performed in a room of the hotel, but who could tell what gross sins might have been committed there?

It was an intensely cold though bright and clear winter morning as the missionaries went out into the narrow, crooked streets crowded with chattering and for the most part squalid Chinese.

Placing themselves in the hands of the Lord to lead them as he saw fit, they walked almost directly to the walls of the "Forbidden City," the former home of emperors and nobility. Entering the gate they walked past shrines, pagodas, and temples fast falling to decay, as all else in China is, and came to a grove of what they took to be cypress trees. A hallowed and reverential feeling was upon them. It was one of those occasions which at rare intervals come to mortals when they are surrounded by a Presence so sacred that human words would be disturbing. The brethren were very sure unseen holy beings were directing their footsteps.

On the way to this grove many people were passed, but the number gradually diminished as they reached its borders. In it only two men were to be seen, and these left almost immediately. There, in the heart of the capital of the most populous nation in the world, unnoticed and undisturbed by the multitudes who were almost within a stone's throw of them, they supplicated the Lord for his blessing, after which Brother McKay offered the dedicatory prayer which in substance was as follows:

"Our Heavenly Father: In deep humility and gratitude, we thy servants approach thee in prayer and supplication on this most solemn and momentous occasion. We pray thee to draw near unto us, to grant us the peace asked for in the opening prayer by Brother Cannon; and to let the channel of communication between thee and us be open, that thy word may be spoken, and thy will be done. We pray for forgiveness of any folly, weakness, or lightmindedness that it may not stand between us and the rich outpouring of thy Holy Spirit. Holy Father, grant us thy peace and thy inspiration, and may we not be disturbed during this solemn service.

"For thy kind protection and watchful care over us in our travels by land and by sea, we render our sincere gratitude. We are grateful, too, for the fellowship and brotherly love we have one for the other, that our hearts beat as one, and that we stand before thee this holy Sabbath day with clean hands, pure hearts, and with our minds free from all worldly cares.

"Though keenly aware of the great responsibility this special mission entails, yet we are thankful that thou hast called us to perform it. Heavenly Father, make us equal, we beseech thee, to every duty and task. As we visit thy Missions in the various parts of the world, give us keen insight into the conditions and needs of each, and bestow upon us in rich abundance the gift of discernment.

"With grateful hearts, we acknowledge thy guiding influence in our travels to this great land of China, and particularly to this quiet and secluded spot in the heart of this ancient and crowded city. We pray that the petition setting this spot apart as a place of prayer and dedication may be granted by thee and that it may be held sacred in thy sight.

"Holy Father, we rejoice in the knowledge of the truth, and in the restoration of the Gospel of the Redeemer. We praise thy name for having revealed thyself and thine Only Begotten Son to thy servant, Joseph the Prophet, and that through thy revelations the Church, in its purity and perfection, was established in these last days for the happiness and eternal salvation of the human family. We thank thee for the Priesthood, which gives men authority to officiate in thy holy name.

"In this land there are millions who know not thee nor thy work, who are bound by the fetters of superstition and false doctrine, and who have never been given the opportunity even of hearing the true message of their Redeemer. Countless millions have died in ignorance of thy plan of life and salvation. We feel deeply impressed with the realization that the time has come when the light of the glorious Gospel should begin to shine through the dense darkness that has enshrouded this nation for ages.

"To this end, therefore, by the authority of the Holy Apostleship, I dedicate and consecrate and set apart the Chinese Realm for the preaching of the Gospel of Jesus Christ as restored in this dispensation through the Prophet Joseph Smith. By this act shall the key be turned that unlocks the door through which thy chosen servants shall enter with glad tidings of great joy to this benighted and senile nation. That their message may be given in peace, we beseech thee, O God, to stabilize the Chinese government. Thou knowest how it is torn with dissension at the present time, and how faction contends against faction to the oppression of the people and the strangling of the nation's life. Holy Father, may peace and stability be established throughout this republic, if not by the present government, then through the intervention of the allied powers of the civilized world.

"Heavenly Father, manifest thy tender mercy toward thy suffering children throughout this famine-stricken realm! Stay the progress of pestilence, and may starvation and untimely death stalk no more through the land. Break the bands of superstition, and may the young men and young women come out of the darkness of the Past into the Glorious Light now shining among the children of men. Grant, our Father, that these young men and women may, through upright, virtuous lives, and prayerful study, be prepared and inclined to declare this message of salvation in their own tongue to their fellowmen. May their hearts, and the hearts of this people, be turned to their fathers that they may accept the opportunity offered them to bring salvation to the millions who have gone before.

"May the Elders and Sisters whom thou shalt call to this land as missionaries have keen insight into the mental and spiritual state of the Chinese mind. Give them special power and ability to approach this people in such a manner as will make the proper appeal to them. We beseech thee, O God, to reveal to thy servants the best methods to adopt and the best plans to follow in establishing thy work among this ancient, tradition-steeped people. May the work prove joyous, and a rich harvest of honest souls bring that peace to the workers' hearts which surpasseth all understanding.

"Remember thy servants, whom thou hast chosen to preside in thy Church. We uphold and sustain before thee President Heber J. Grant, who stands at the head at this time, and his counselors, President Anthon H. Lund and President Charles W. Penrose. Bless them, we pray thee, with every needful blessing, and keep them one in all things pertaining to thy work. Likewise bless the Council of Twelve. May they continue to be one with the First Presidency. Remember the Presiding Patriarch, the First Council of Seventy, the

Presiding Bishopric, and all who preside in stakes, wards, quorums, organizations, temples, Church schools, and missions. May the spirit of purity, peace, and energy characterize all thy organizations.

"Heavenly Father, be kind to our Loved Ones from whom we are now separated. Let thy Holy Spirit abide in our homes, that sickness, disease, and death may not enter therein.

"Hear us, O kind and Heavenly Father, we implore thee, and open the door for the preaching of thy Gospel from one end of this realm to the other, and may thy servants who declare this message be especially blest and directed by thee. May thy kingdom come, and thy will be done speedily here on earth among all peoples, kindreds ,and tongues preparatory to the winding up scenes of these latter days!

"And while we behold thy guiding hand through it all, we shall ascribe unto thee the praise, the glory, and the honor, through Jesus Christ our Lord and Redeemer, Amen."

The brethren felt that this prayer was acceptable to the Almighty. His spirit gave approving testimony and at the same time revealed for their comfort and blessing some things which should transpire in the future.

Poor old China, the victim of intrigues among nations who covet her coal and iron deposits, the victim of floods and droughts, of famines and pestilence, and worst of all, the victim of her own inefficiency and helplessness! Assuredly she needs someone to plead her cause before the throne of grace. China is living in the dead past of two thousand years and has hardly begun to realize it.

And still her condition is not hopeless. She is as one passing through travail. A new nation, let us hope, is being born, a nation of great potential power, with leaders sufficiently wise to develop and properly exploit her natural resources. Among this people are hosts of splendid individuals, men and women of stable character, of refinement and intelligence. That many of them will accept the truth when it is presented to them cannot be doubted, if one may judge from the faithful Latter-day Saints of that race who have joined the Church in Hawaii and Samoa.

This chapter should not be closed without expressing the hope that should any reader of these lines be called to labor as a missionary in that land he will not feel he is going among a people who are unworthy of his efforts. He will find there castes and outcasts, but among both will be found men and women who will prove a credit to the Church.

Cypress Garden in the Forbidden City, Peking
(now Beijing), China, Where China was
Dedicated for the Preaching of the Gospel

President Hugh J. Cannon at Great Wall, China

CHAPTER 6

EXPERIENCES
IN CHINA

"The vice of our theology is seen in the claim that the
Bible is a closed book, and that the age of inspiration is
past."

— Ralph Waldo Emerson

American poet, essayist, Harvard scholar [handwritten annotation]

1803–1882 [handwritten annotation]

On the day following the dedication of China for the preaching
of the Gospel, a visit was made to Charles R. Crane, United States
Ambassador. Mr. Crane, an affable and intelligent gentleman, proved
to be somewhat familiar with the history of the "Mormon" people.
He made the statement that they could make a distinct and valuable
contribution to China's advancement because of their successful
experience in redeeming arid regions.

Mr. Crane spoke feelingly of conditions prevailing in that
distressed land where fifteen million people were facing starvation
and must inevitably meet this fate, he said, unless help came from the
outside. It was reported that in some districts men were killing their
wives and, what is infinitely more horrible, selling their daughters
into shameful slavery to avoid seeing them tortured by hunger.

Think of what the perfectly organized Church of Jesus Christ
could do for this people! Presumably more than four hundred
million had enough to eat, while fifteen million were starving. Had

those with sufficient food accepted and obeyed the simple practice of fasting one day each month and given the food thus saved to the poor, and this had been distributed without cost, as the Lord wills it should be through his organization, the fifteen million sufferers would have had two meals a day for a month, by which time another fast day would have rolled around and furnished them with an additional thirty days' supply. Well might the Lord say, "For as the heavens are higher than the earth, so are my ways higher than your ways, and my thoughts than your thoughts" (Isaiah 55:9).

Pride in the ability to speak a foreign language is rather universal. Often this ability resembles the 180th meridian—purely imaginary. In Japan a milk cart bore the illuminating inscription "Virtuous Milk." Well, why shouldn't it? Virtue denotes purity. Another sign read, "Photographer executed." Upon approaching the elevator of their hotel in Peking, the special missionaries saw written in bold letters, "No Raisins." For a moment they were nonplussed, then it occurred to them that "raisin'" is an elevator's chief occupation. The power was off in the next hotel at which the missionaries stopped and the sign on the elevator there read, "No Currents."

However, it is not to be supposed that these people lack in ability as linguists. In apparent contradiction to what has been said, Chinese speak excellent English, and on the main lines of travel the stranger may go to a ticket office and state his needs with every assurance of being understood. A visit to the Peking Teachers' College, maintained by the government, aroused wonderment. Those who believe the Chinese are a degraded and ignorant people should have been with this party. Native boys were studying college subjects and in several classes were using English textbooks. The president of this college is a graduate of Columbia University, and the professor who showed the visitors around spoke their language almost faultlessly.

An entire book should be written about the great Chinese wall or it should be dismissed with a line or two. Brother McKay and his companion viewed it from Ching-lung-Chiao and at the expense of some energy climbed to the highest point of the wall anywhere near the village and were richly rewarded for the effort. It would reach farther than from Salt Lake City to Chicago and has stood for more than two thousand years, formerly an insurmountable barrier to the invading hordes of Tartar tribes. It twists and writhes over the desolate and barren mountains like a ponderous serpent.

Leaving Peking by train, the missionaries had a good opportunity to compare the courtesy of a Chinese gentleman with that of a European traveler, and to the shame of the white race the comparison was altogether in favor of the so-called heathen. This gentleman, evidently wealthy, was accompanied by his son and a host of servants. With charming courtesy, they had the servants bring to each of the missionaries a cup of tea and cigarettes. The visitors endeavored to show appreciation for the thoughtfulness though declining their offerings.

The route from Peking to Shanghai leads through Tientsin, a city of a million people and the seaport of North China. When our travelers alighted from the train and showed a disposition to take rickshas, the men fought so ferociously for the chance to earn a fare that policemen, with clubs about three feet long and as thick as a very heavy cane, actually beat them off as they would a pack of yelping wolves, which indeed they resembled more than human beings. Though the insistent attention of these creatures was extremely annoying, one could not suppress a feeling of deep sympathy for them. They appeared willing to work, but the opportunity of earning a few cents was evidently rare.

It is thirty-two hours with a fast train from Tientsin to Shanghai, and the route runs through the edge of the Shantung province, one of the districts most affected by the famine. Even from the railroad many heartrending sights were to be seen. Millions of people live in mud hovels, less habitable than the Indian tepee.

But the zenith of primitive living was seen on the boats at Pukow, where the famed Yangtze river was crossed on a ferry plying between that city and Nanking. On these boats or rafts children are born, reared, married, raise their own families and die. Almost their first visit ashore, and certainly their last, is when they are carried out and buried in some mound in a barren field.

As has been stated, the impelling motive in writing an account of this tour is to bear witness of the goodness of the Lord to those who depend upon him. On one occasion President Wilford Woodruff was heard to say to a departing missionary, "When you need clothes or food or a bed just tell the Lord and he will supply it." Of course these words are true, for they merely state in slightly different form a positive promise of the Master himself, a promise often put to the test by members of this Church.

This special missionary party had reason to know that the Almighty always does his full part. Their train arrived in Shanghai at eleven p.m. and though reservations had been made in advance through the hotel in Peking, no accommodations were available. People were occupying chairs in the lobbies of every respectable hotel in the city. But the Lord had been asked to open the way for his servants, and after some delay the clerk concluded it would be possible to put cots in the ladies' drawing room; and this he did upon being assured that the missionaries would be up and dressed early on the following morning.

They learned the next day from an American doctor that he had been obliged to sleep on a billiard table with his overcoat as a pillow and with no bedding, though he was a frequent patron of this hotel and felt he had a "pull" there. It is a significant fact, too, that he arrived at the hotel before they did. The following evening the brethren had a comfortable room to themselves.

There is an incongruous mixture of Occidental civilization and Oriental primitiveness in Shanghai. Unlike Peking, the city has a street car system and other modern means of transportation. On some of the streets the visitor would think he was in Europe; on others not ten minutes distant he might easily imagine himself in the innermost heart of China.

A most delightful voyage is that from Shanghai to Kobe, Japan. For many miles the sea is discolored by the muddy waters of the Yellow and the Yangtze Rivers. The first Japanese point to be reached was Nagasaki, famous as the chief coal loading station of the Far East. Here man power seems to be the cheapest thing on the market, and the largest steamers are loaded by hand. This operation furnishes one of the sights for which Nagasaki is famous. A number of barges come alongside the vessel and from these a series of platforms are built to the deck. Workers are stationed on each platform and the coal is passed from one to the other in baskets which contain about twenty-five pounds of coal. Men and women, boys and girls are engaged in this work. And how they do work! These baskets are passed from one person to the next with surprising rapidity, each line of people sending up about fifty baskets per minute, and there were enough lines working to put on about 500 tons per hour. They worked loading the *Tenyo Maru* from five o'clock in the morning until late that afternoon, though they had put three thousand tons into another ship during the night. In spite of this they were a merry and apparently lighthearted crowd, but signs of fatigue were evident before their task was completed. On one occasion when rushed for time, 5,500 tons of coal was loaded into one vessel in seven hours.

It would be worth a trip across the Pacific to see this beautiful landlocked harbor, with the green terraced slopes, the unique and picturesque houses lining the water and extending to the tops of the surrounding hills, the quaint water craft of every description including gondolas much resembling though not so beautiful as the Venetians.

The missionaries went ashore for a few hours and walked to the summit of one of the scenic hills. The houses, as is customary in Japan, are crowded close together, and inasmuch as they are all open, the visitor feels he is intruding into the privacy of the family; but there was evidence that no privacy exists, nor do the people desire it. The Europeans, with their strange clothes and manners, were a source of interest and amusement to the native children who had quite as much enjoyment out of it as the strangers did.

From Nagasaki to Kobe the vessel steams through the Inland Sea. The mainland is visible on one side, and on the other are numerous mountainous islands, making the scene most picturesque and delightful. The water was as pacific as one could expect it to be from its name. One wonders how a comparatively few miles can make such a vast difference as is to be seen between Japan and China. One country is fertile and green and the other is most desolate. Naturally southern China is less austere, but there is little difference in latitude between Japan and that part of China which Brother McKay visited.

When pulling up to the wharf at Kobe, the vessel bumped into the concrete wall. Apparently this was not serious, but nevertheless it was destined to play a part in the brethren's plans.

The trip from Kobe to Tokyo was made by rail, as the passengers have the option of continuing with the boat or going overland and rejoining it at Yokohama. The missionaries again stopped off in Osaka and with the elders laboring there went to Kyoto, which is one of the most beautiful of all Japanese cities.

The sleeping cars in China and Japan are arranged on much the same order as are European day coaches, in compartments. These are very convenient when one is fortunate enough to secure a compartment alone or when the other occupants are of an agreeable sort; but when one has an upper berth and the man underneath smokes at least three times during the night, as was the case on this trip, it is far from pleasant.

This same smoker jumped simultaneously out of his bed and his kimono, which answered for pajamas, and wholly unadorned went through certain setting-up exercises, paying no more attention to fellow travelers or to the men and women who passed the open door than they paid to him. Indeed, a very fine looking young woman stepped into the doorway in order to permit a gentleman to pass her in the narrow corridor; but she and the unadorned man were equally unconcerned.

Mention has been made of the crowded condition of the hotels. The ships traveling eastward were likewise unable to care for the traffic at this season, and considerable difficulty was had in securing accommodations at all. While in Shanghai efforts in this direction had been made, and the travelers finally succeeded in being booked in a cabin for three, the other occupant being a Chinese, who was to come aboard at Yokohama.

En route to Tokyo, Brother McKay asked Brother Cannon to stop off at Yokohama to see if he could not secure a cabin for two. At first the company courteously but positively declared this to be wholly impossible, but before Brother Cannon left the office the desired accommodations had been obtained, and the hand of the Lord was acknowledged in this matter, for the company declined to make any additional charge.

The skeptical reader will see nothing miraculous in this incident and will attribute it to chance, but these things occurred with such frequency during this tour that to give credit to chance or to any earthly power would be ungrateful. Chance does not discriminate between missionaries and other travelers, and on this and many subsequent occasions these brethren secured accommodations which even the steamship companies said could not possibly be had.

While in China and en route back to Japan, Brother McKay was concerned because he felt he should have two days more in which to complete the work in that land. But his plans seemed to demand that he sail with the *Tenyo Maru* as this was the only vessel which would take his party to Hawaii early enough to keep up with the outlined program. Brother Lloyd O. Ivie, the newly appointed president of the Japanese Mission, was expected on the next boat and it was desirable that Brother McKay should be present and arrange for the transfer of presidency and give such instructions as he might deem proper.

However, the *Tenyo Maru* was scheduled to sail without giving the opportunity of seeing Brother Ivie, or making other needed arrangements. The brethren, though disappointed, prepared to leave at the scheduled time, but learned after all their packing had been done that the apparently insignificant bump received by the vessel in Kobe was sufficiently serious to demand two days delay, exactly the time needed, while the damage was being repaired.

Brother Ivie did not arrive as expected, but this extra time was sufficient for Brother McKay to make proper arrangements for the care of the mission after President Stimpson left, he having already been released and his passage to the United States engaged and paid for; so that while the accident was an inconvenient one for the steamship company and most of the passengers and resulted in the discharge of the captain, it was a fortunate one for the missionaries.

The visit to these lands was delightfully interesting. The Japanese are looking for the best in everything, in science, in inventions, in government, in ships, in machinery; and it seems reasonable to expect that some day they will begin looking for the best in religion. But the sham and sophistry, the mass of error put forth under the label of Christ's holy Church will not satisfy their critical minds, and has added to the suspicion with which they view foreign beliefs.

Most of the nations of the earth were represented at the wharf when the time finally came for the *Tenyo Maru* to leave for San Francisco via Hawaii. It was a perfect bedlam. The band was playing, porters were hurrying aboard with luggage, mail wagons were forcing their way through crowds, bringing the last mail to the vessel.

As the boat moved slowly from the pier, most of those on board threw rolls of colored paper to friends on shore, retaining one end themselves until there was a gorgeous mass of streamers connecting vessel with land. As the ship pulled out, the papers were unrolled and were so long that they extended some distance into the harbor, their own weight finally breaking them. It was a beautiful symbol of the ties which bind those departing to loved ones, and of the heartstrings which are broken when the parting hour arrives.

The *Tenyo Maru*. This Ship Had an Accident, Causing a Two-Day Delay, Enabling the Brethren to Finish Their Work in China.

CHAPTER 7

OAHU AND MAUI ISLANDS OF HAWAII

"In my labors as a missionary, it was much easier for me to ask the Lord for what I needed than to ask of man; and the Almighty never failed to hear."

— George Q. Cannon

It seemed hardly possible that the new world which our travelers entered at the harbor of Honolulu is on the same globe as the cheerless one seen at China. This was truly a fairyland. Palms, ferns, flowers, and luxuriant tropical foliage all contribute their part toward making this a terrestrial paradise. But before driving along the beach, which was lined with coconut palms, always leaning toward the sea, and with the stately royal palms, as straight as any arrow ever made, visitors must steam into the harbor at the entrance to which they are met by a crowd of boys and young men in the water who swim about the vessel and dive for coins thrown overboard by prodigal passengers.

President E. Wesley Smith met Brother McKay's party at the pier and, after Sister Kamohalii, a native member, had placed leis about their necks in behalf of the sisters of the branch, he took them to the very beautiful Mission Home, where Sister Smith, the children, and Elders Lee Van Wagoner and Rowland Browning and Sisters

Wealthy Clark and Ivy May Frazier extended hospitable welcome.

Hawaii furnishes a page of important missionary history. Among the first company sent to this land was George Q. Cannon. A few years later Joseph F. Smith, at the time only fifteen years old, also went to this field. Though not on the islands at the same time, it was largely due to mutual interest in the natives that they first became well acquainted. Subsequently they labored together in the Quorum of Twelve and for more than a score of years were associated as counselors in the First Presidency and loved each other with all their intense natures.

It seemed fitting that a son of each of these men should be present during the meetings held in Hawaii by Brother McKay. More than once during the visit it was felt that the spirits of these departed leaders were present, and some experiences were had which are too sacred to publish to the world.

The Hawaiian Islands offer almost as good a demonstration of Japanese life as does Japan itself, and there are so many Chinese residing there that except for the beautiful surroundings the visitor might easily think he was in China. At the time of this visit the Hawaiian Territorial Board of Health gave out figures which indicated that the pure native blood was being replaced by that of more vigorous nations. Of the 263,666 inhabitants, 159,900 were listed as Asiatics, divided as follows: 110,000 Japanese, 22,800 Chinese, 5,100 Koreans, and 22,000 Filipinos. There are also many Portuguese on the islands as well as representatives from almost every nation under the sun.

At Laie, about thirty-five miles from Honolulu, the Church owns a rather large and productive plantation, a considerable part of which is devoted to sugarcane and pineapple culture. The temple is located here, and a school is also maintained by the Church. One of Brother McKay's especial duties was to visit our schools, and some little time was spent in this beautiful place.

The children in attendance at this institution ranged in age from seven to fourteen years. They were under the direction of William T. Cannon, Jr., who was acting as principal, assisted by Mary S.

Christensen, Evelyn Olson, Edythe L. Bell, Jane Jenkins, Genevieve Hammond, and Elizabeth Hyde, all missionaries giving their time gratuitously to this work.

Children and teachers formed in line and participated in the flag raising ceremonies. When all was in readiness, little William Kaaa, a full-blooded Hawaiian, stepped from the ranks and said:

"Hats off!
Along the street there comes
A blare of bugles,
A ruffle of drums,
A flash of color beneath the sky,
Hats off!
The flag is passing by."

Then Master Marr Waddoups, a young American, repeated:

"Now raise the starry banner up,
Emblem of our country's glory,
And teach the children of this land
Its grave and wondrous story;
Of how in early times it waved
High o'er the Continentals,
Who fought and made our country free,
The one true home of liberty."

Next came a Japanese boy, Otockochi Matsumoto:

"Salute the flag, oh children,
With grave and reverent hand,
For it means far more than the eye can see,
Your home and your native land.
And many have died for its crimson bars,
Its field of blue with the spangled stars."

At the conclusion of this verse, the entire school, including teachers and visitors, saluted the flag:

"I pledge allegiance to my flag and to the republic for which it stands; one nation indivisible, with liberty and justice for all."

This done, William Kaaa again stepped forward, and the ceremony was concluded with the following:

"This flag that now waves o'er our school,
Protecting weak and strong,
Is the flag that vindicates the right
And punishes the wrong."

In the group participating in these exercises were Hawaiians, Americans, Chinese, Japanese, Portuguese, and Filipinos, and possibly some other nationalities.

America is indeed a "Melting Pot" and, aided by the Gospel, it can make one people of all nations.

A pleasant duty of the special missionaries was to visit the temple, at that time presided over by Brother William M. Waddoups, who has since been made president of the mission. Before doing so, however, they had breakfast with the family, and Sister Waddoups proved herself not only a devoted missionary but an excellent cook as well. Though this was on February 7th, the visitors were furnished with all the freshly picked strawberries they could eat, and around this home and on adjoining land banana trees were growing in profusion.

In traveling by auto from Honolulu to Laie the usual course passes over the Pali, one of the real scenic spots of the world. From this elevated point one can look into a valley where many thousands of acres are producing bounteous crops of pineapples and sugarcane. And beyond is the sea. A paved road zigzags like a great serpent from this spot down the steep mountainside and into the valley. A majestic mountain towers above the Pali on one side and a precipice yawns on the other, and around this point a perfect hurricane constantly sweeps. It frequently blows the tops off autos and it is impossible for even a strong man to stand erect. Strangely enough the wind is felt only at one spot; thirty feet distant it is perfectly calm.

No visitor among the Polynesians is likely ever to forget the feasts which are prepared and set before him. As the Hawaiians do not often have the opportunity of entertaining one of the general authorities of the Church, they were anxious to make Brother McKay's stay among them pleasant. The tables were usually covered with a cloth of ferns and at the outset literally groaned with the loads they bore. The aim of the natives is to transfer the load and consequent groaning to the visitor.

One breakfast served to the special missionaries consisted of beef, eggs, shrimps, several kinds of fish, various vegetables, fruits of all kinds, chicken, the characteristic Hawaiian poi, bread, French toast, green onions, and pie, and all in almost limitless quantities. If that is a breakfast, the imagination is inclined to balk if asked to conjure up a dinner.

During this visit a Honolulu paper printed a news item of unique interest to people from the semi-arid west. L.H. Daingerfield, meteorologist in charge of the U.S. weather bureau at Waialeale, on the island of Kauai, certifies that from January 7, 1920 to February 3, 1921, at least 590 inches of rain fell. With such an abundance of moisture and a tropical climate one can easily understand why the country is so green and beautiful.

Brother McKay's party, in company with President E. Wesley Smith, visited the island of Maui where they were welcomed by Elders Byron D. Jones, Samuel H. Hurst, Leslie Dunn, Chester H. Nelson, and Lester Williams and two native elders, David Keola Kailimai and David Kalani.

This island means much to the Church, for here missionary work among the dark-skinned people was really started. December 23, 1850, a company of ten missionaries landed in Honolulu from Utah. The youngest member of the party was George Q. Cannon. They had worked their way across the desert from Utah to San Francisco, then in the height of the gold fever, and had earned sufficient money in California to engage passage to the islands. The Elder in charge of the party became discouraged and decided to return home, but this suggestion was wholly contrary to Brother Cannon's feelings. He was in a peculiar position. Obedience to those presiding over him was a cardinal part of his nature, but he could not feel that it was right to leave the field because difficulties, howsoever insurmountable they appeared, confronted them. As many months must elapse before an answer could be expected from Salt Lake he submitted the matter to the Lord, promising that he would do whatever was desired of him if he could but know the wishes of the Almighty.

Fifty years later, and but a few months before his death, he again visited the islands at the great Jubilee which was held in the fall of 1900. After his return to Salt Lake, he met with his family and related some experiences of his life and particularly of his recent trip. His impressive words were those of an honest man who knew his earthly days were numbered and who desired to leave final testimony as a legacy to his posterity. After relating many details of his visit and the memories which it awakened, he said in effect:

"We were riding in a carriage with President Samuel E. Woolley when we came to a spot which to me was very sacred. Leaving the others behind and with the request that I should not be disturbed, I walked into a garden among the banyan and banana trees and stood on the spot where I, as a young and inexperienced man beset by problems which I myself could not solve, had pleaded with the Lord for guidance, promising him I would do his will if he would but reveal it to me. There in that garden, the Lord talked with me as one man talks to another, telling me I should remain, for a great work was to be done among that people."

It was with chastened spirits that Brother McKay and his party went over this ground. All about them were evidences of the fulfillment of the promise that a mighty work was to be done among those lovable and honest-hearted souls. This point was emphasized by an interview which Brother McKay, in company with Brothers Smith and Cannon, had with Dr. Louis R. Sullivan, anthropologist in charge of the British Museum in Honolulu and the man who was directing a number of scientists in an endeavor to trace a relationship between the various Polynesian races and the American Indians.

During an interview with this courteous and learned gentleman, Brother McKay said:

"Dr. Sullivan, you have examined the Hawaiians as a scientist, have been in their homes, have conversed with and questioned them, have made numerous physical examinations and now know your subject. How do the 'Mormons' among these people compare with the others?"

The doctor answered instantly:

"You have the cream of the islands." Then he proceeded: "I do not know whether what you have appeals to the best natives, or whether you take them as they come and make the best out of them. But certain it is that you have the best now."

It was in Wailuku, on the island of Maui, that the Book of Mormon was translated and where that faithful man lived, Brother Jonatana H. Napela, who rendered such valuable assistance to this work and whose name is so often mentioned in "My First Mission," written by George Q. Cannon. The visiting brethren had the pleasure of meeting his grandson, Brother Titus Parker.

Elder Kailimai's Ford was at the disposal of the visitors and in it they rode out to visit and have dinner with some members of the Church who live far up on the side of Haleakala, the largest extinct volcano in the world. From here they drove to Pulehu, where George Q. Cannon and Brother Napela had preached with such power that 97 of the 100 people who came to hear them were converted. The tradition is that Brother Cannon was not standing on the ground on this occasion, but was in the air and that a great light shone about him.

Under a beautiful tree on the lot where this occurred and where the Church now has a neat little chapel, the visiting brethren engaged in prayer. It was an occasion which none of them will ever forget, for they stood almost in the visible presence of celestial beings. In looking back on the trip after the lapse of several years, there are few, if any, experiences which are more impressive than this. [See Appendix B.]

Aboard the *Mauna Kea* which was to convey the party to Hilo, on the island of Hawaii, the missionaries met a wealthy gentleman from Salt Lake who was touring the islands with his wife. Being acquainted with these people, the brethren were soon engaged in conversation with them and Brother Cannon said:

"Through that canyon my father walked seventy years ago. He was young and inexperienced, without food, friends, money, or suitable clothing, and without the language. Indeed, almost the only thing he did possess was a sublime faith in the thing he had come to do. While attempting to cross a stream he had fallen into the water and presented a bedraggled and poverty-stricken appearance, but the Almighty gave to some influential people, whose home he passed, the impression to go out and meet him. Among those who thus came was a prominent native judge, a man noted for his learning and goodness. Through this meeting he and his family came into the Church, and he was of great assistance in translating the Book of Mormon into the Hawaiian language." The man who met and befriended the forlorn looking youth was Brother Napela referred to above.

Pulehu Chapel, Maui, Hawaii. This is the Sacred
Spot Mentioned on Page 61 and in Appendix B

CHAPTER 8

HAWAII AND KAUAI ISLANDS

"Thou wilt shew me the path of life: in thy presence is fulness of joy; at thy right hand there are pleasures for evermore."

—Psalm 16:11

The ride from Lahaina, on the island of Maui, to Hilo, on the island of Hawaii, is a very beautiful one. The sea and the distant islands were especially attractive between daybreak and sunrise. Overshadowing the boat towered the highest mountain in the Pacific, Mauna Kea, 14,000 feet high, snow-capped and blushing because of the kiss which it, in view of curious spectators, was receiving from the sun. Silvery flying fish were rising from the water and at no great distance several whales could be seen.

As the visiting party approached the conference house in Hilo several missionaries were busy with grubbing hoes in the yard. They were clearing out the weeds, which in this instance were banana plants, an excellent illustration of the truth that the choicest plants, like human beings, are weeds if they do not remain within their own bounds.

Edwin K. Winder, a grandson of that stalwart Church worker President John R. Winder, was in charge of this district, and his wife, a granddaughter of President George Q. Cannon, was matron of the conference house; and the welcome extended the visitors was a heartfelt one.

Hawaii is the largest island of this group and one of the most productive. Thousands and thousands of acres of sugarcane grow without irrigation. Through many of these plantations there are cemented waterways, and a strong head of water carries the cane to the mills, instead of the usual method being followed which is to lay a portable track through the fields and run a small engine and train of cars direct from field to mill.

Attending the missionary meeting, which was held in Hilo, besides the visiting brethren, were President Winder and his wife, Alma Cannon Winder, Sister Virginia Budd, and Elders Roscoe C. Cox, Ben E. Swan, Boyd C. Davis, Milo F. Kirkham, James W. Miller, Leland N. Goff, Leslie F. Stone, and George M. Bronson. These missionaries, not one of whom was much past his majority and some of whom were not yet out of their teens, were laboring with courage and devotion among this dark-skinned people, and their testimonies indicated that they were finding unspeakable joy in their work.

So interesting was this meeting that a veritable banquet was forgotten, and a good family with their host of assembled friends was kept waiting. Among the company was the most famous string quartet on the islands. And how these boys did sing and play! Their happy faces, sparkling eyes, the skill of their fingers and beauty of their voices are no more to be described than was the meal itself, consisting as it did of every kind of tropical fruit and everything else which a bounteous land produces and which willing and apt hands could prepare.

More than three hundred eager people awaited the arrival of the visitors in the comfortable chapel. As is customary they all arose as the brethren entered and remained standing until the visitors had taken their seats. The joy of these people in meeting one of the general Church authorities was thoroughly genuine and was akin to that which redeemed souls will have when they gaze upon the face and hear the voice of the Redeemer.

Preach my Gospel

"Man is that he might have joy." This is not merely a privilege which mortals may accept or reject at will. It is a duty. And the Hawaiians set their white co-religionists a worthy example by finding in their worship the most exquisite joy known to man, and which after all is a foretaste of future heavenly joy.

Space will not permit of reference to every feast, either of a spiritual or mundane nature, given to Brother McKay's party, but those which are briefly mentioned here are typical of all the others.

Thirty-seven miles from Hilo is Kilauea, the largest active volcano in the world, so colossal that it makes the time-honored and destructive Vesuvius boil and sputter with furious envy. After the meeting referred to above, nine missionaries were taken in Fords owned by local members to this seething inferno. During the remainder of the night and until after sunrise next morning the visitors walked about the crater and were awed by its greatness. In some places the lava might easily have been reached with a walking stick were it not for the intense heat which forbids too close an approach. There are rivers and lakes of molten material, bubbling, hissing, and performing weird and fantastic tricks. Huge masses of the fiery substance are being constantly thrown into the air in the most grotesque and monstrous forms, as though they had been spewed from the mouth of some herculean monster. At times the sulphurous fumes are almost overpowering, and there seemed justification for the statement made by one of the party that it was hell itself. He added that as a result of the numerous feasts which had been crowded upon him he felt exactly like the volcano.

No greater contrast can be imagined than that offered by Kilauea and that which meets the gaze as one descends into the valley. Behind, wrathful purgatory; in front, attractive Elysium foliage, the distant picturesque town and the exquisite blue ocean as a background make a scene so impressively beautiful that the fortunate visitor feels it can never be effaced from memory.

Many tears were shed as good-bye was said when the missionary party embarked for Honolulu. The brethren were almost smothered in leis, and their own eyes were moist as they bade farewell to these affectionate people.

Some months before this tour was planned, Elder George Bowles, now bishop of Belvedere Ward, his wife Christine A., and his son George A. accepted a call to go to the Hawaiian Islands. Before leaving Salt Lake he had a dream in which he saw the special visitors on the islands. So impressive was this manifestation that he told some of his friends he would surely see these particular brethren in Hawaii, though at that time nothing seemed less likely.

The special missionaries had the pleasure, in company with Elder Wilford J. Cole, of riding on horseback over the beautiful plantation at Laie owned by the Church and which he was then managing.

A number of missionaries devote a part of their time in assisting President Waddoups with the temple work. Among those thus engaged were John L. Larson, Arnold B. Chrystal, Arnold B. Bangerter and his wife, Hazel N. Bangerter, David J. Smith, and J. Clair Anderson.

After visiting the islands of Oahu, on which Honolulu is located, and Maui and Hawaii, one can hardly imagine anything more like a garden; and still it is said the island of Kauai is the real garden of the group. A visit was made to this place, and the travelers were inclined to agree that this claim was not without foundation. The landing was made at 3:30 in the morning at Nawiliwili. The steamer anchored outside the breakwater and passengers went ashore in small rowboats. The sky was as black as ink and the darkness and uncanny swish of oars through the water made the traveler feel that the silent boatman was taking him on his fateful journey across the river Styx.

Church members on this island have purchased a Ford and given it to the missionaries, as two Elders have the entire island to cover. Brother Lloyd D. Davis met the visitors at the wharf with this machine, and the way they traveled over the island visiting friends and members and keeping appointments for meeting was a poor example to set for those who live in a country where speed regulations must be observed.

There were few places visited on this world tour which will withstand the dimming effect of passing years longer than will "Beach House" on this island. It is the home of a Mr. McBryde, a very wealthy man and good friend of our people. Though the house itself is simple, the white sandy beach, the placid bay, lawns, beautiful flowers, coconut and royal palms, evergreens, the purple and pink bougainvilleas, so profuse as to make a perfectly gorgeous sight, all combined to make the place little short of enchanting.

Not far from this attractive home is the "spouting horn." A jutting ledge of lava rock reaches to the ocean. In this rock there was evidently a seam softer than the rest and during past ages waves have bored a long hole which comes to the surface about fifty feet from the sea. The breakers come in with such irresistible force that the water is driven through this hole and spouts from fifty to a hundred feet in the air, resembling Old Faithful in Yellowstone in everything except regularity.

The missionary meeting which convened in Honolulu was, if possible, the most inspirational of any held on these islands. There were in attendance Elders Ora C. Barlow, Kenneth C. Weaver, Ferrin R. Harris, Douglas F. Budd, John Parker, Joseph F. Smith, son of the late Hyrum M. Smith, Leroy E. Carroll, A. Harris Chase, Adelbert Barnett, Wallace H. Penrose, grandson of the late President Charles W. Penrose, Robert Plunkett, and Heber A. Amussen, and some others whose names are recorded elsewhere in this chronicle.

Their names are mentioned for a special reason. It has often been claimed by enemies of the Church that, though older Mormons might stubbornly adhere to their belief, young men and women of the second, third, and fourth generations would not be so true. Among the hundreds of representatives of the Church whom these special missionaries met during this tour, there were very few who belonged to the first generation. Most of them belonged to the third, fourth, and many to the fifth. All of them had the opportunity of bearing their testimony and did so with a fervor which emphatically belied the claim referred to above. The special missionaries did not ask the Elders what generation in the Church they represented, but since that time the author of these lines has put the question to 391 missionaries in different fields with the following results: first generation, 16; second, 37; third, 151; fourth, 163; fifth, 24.

Missionary fields as well as the work at home give irrefutable proof that "Mormonism" is "carrying on," and that every prediction made concerning its growth and stability is being fulfilled. The false prophets are those who predicted its disintegration, the true ones those who foresaw and foretold its success.

The last of the meetings in Hawaii was held in that delightful spot, Laie. It was a busy Sabbath day. The Sunday School, presided over by Brother Charles J. Broad, was a very creditable one. For nine years Brother Broad was superintendent of the school in Honolulu and during that period he was never once late, and the only time he was absent was when his son lay dead in his home.

As soon after landing in Honolulu from Japan as it was possible for Brother McKay to decide when he would be ready to leave, efforts were made to secure accommodations on board a vessel for San Francisco, as the steamers here were even more crowded than those farther westward. No hopes were held out that berths could be secured for several weeks, but these missionaries were on the Lord's business. Brother McKay had made appointments ahead which must be filled or serious disappointment would result.

As his work on the islands neared completion, a slight hope was extended that the required accommodations could be had, but the company was far from positive in their statements. However, all preparations were made to leave, even to the farewell which was held in the grounds of the Mission Home.

This was an unforgettable evening, the most beautiful that the author of these lines has ever seen. In the house and gardens were 450 people, among them a number of friends who had not yet joined the Church. The Royal Hawaiian Band, led by Major Kealakai, who has achieved distinction as a leader in Europe, as well as in his native land, was in attendance. These musicians had come voluntarily because of the esteem in which our people are held and because several members of the band are our own "Mormon" boys.

In addition to the band there were a number of noted vocalists and instrumentalists present. It is surprising how quickly the Hawaiian music takes hold of one's heart, and it was especially easy for it to do so on this occasion. In an exquisitely beautiful tropical garden under the bluest sky and the brightest of full moons imaginable the touching "Aloha Oe" sung by the natives and accompanied by their sweet and plaintive stringed instruments was irresistible.

At the conclusion of the evening's program, Brother McKay dedicated the Mission Home.

The good-byes, regretfully and in many cases tearfully said, lasted far into the night. Then the packing had to be done, for late that afternoon the steamship company had said that berths of some kind would be furnished. Scarcely were the travelers safely tucked under the indispensable mosquito netting, a most necessary precaution to take in this and other tropical countries, when strains of sweet music greeted their ears. A quartet of native brethren serenaders sang and played, and one can hardly imagine anything musical which would be more affecting.

The farewells and music were all repeated the following morning as the special missionaries were ready to go aboard their vessel, and in addition leis were hung about their necks until they were almost buried. So bedecked were they that when they went aboard several of the passengers asked them to stand while Kodak pictures were taken, and one man said, "Don't you fellows feel lonesome out in the world like this without any friends?"

Through a Mr. Hardeman who was aboard and whom the brethren had met en route to Japan, the passengers soon learned that Brother McKay was a "Mormon" Apostle, but this seemed to make no difference in the friendship which they manifested.

In Hawaii there are about eleven thousand Church members and they equal in devotion and faith the Latter-day Saints anywhere in the world. Indeed, in the matter of faith, one might almost say they are superior to most other Church members. In all Polynesian islands one sees that childlike and effective trust which was exhibited by the two thousand young Lamanites of whom we read in the 56th and following chapters of Alma in the Book of Mormon.

It is hardly too much to say that all natives of these islands know the doctrines taught by this Church are true, and the sole reason why all, or nearly all, do not accept the truth is that they are not willing or lack the moral strength to obey its strict teachings. It frequently happens that a baptized member, who has indulged his appetite for tobacco or liquor, will refuse to open a meeting with prayer because he is oppressed by the consciousness of unworthiness.

In the summer of 1920, a company of New Zealanders came to Hawaii for the purpose of doing temple work. Two of these brethren whose homes were far apart had no opportunity of comparing genealogies until they reached Laie. There, a comparison showed that they both were descended from a Hawaiian chief, Nameal Hema, who lived more than a thousand years ago. Later it was discovered that several Hawaiian families also traced their records back to this same Hema. Dates and names leave no doubt that this chief is the common ancestor of many families in both countries.

Dr. Sullivan, already referred to, was directing an expedition of scientists who were endeavoring to trace the relationship of the different Polynesian peoples and to connect them if possible, with the American Indians. At the time of Brother McKay's visit this gentleman seemed to be certain of the relationship, though he stated that it was not yet a scientifically demonstrated fact.

Hawaii is called the "Come Back Land." Even if there were no contributing causes, the country itself would justify the designation. But when to the physical beauty of the place is added the music, the deep and touching love of the people, the joy they manifest at meeting, and the sincere sorrow at parting, it is easy to understand how appropriately it could be thus named.

CHAPTER 9

BLESSINGS RECEIVED

"A miracle simply means a phenomenon that is not understood."

—John A. Widtsoe

As was expected, the *Maui*, on which the special missionaries took passage for San Francisco, was very much crowded. They had been anxious to obtain a cabin to themselves in order better to prepare and consider the reports of their visit to China, Japan, and Hawaii which should be made to the general authorities. Instead of obtaining the desired accommodations, however, they were in separate cabins, each with two other men as fellow travelers. Upon boarding the vessel, the purser was visited in an effort to change this arrangement, but he said:

"Were it not for the fact that we do so much business with your people, you could not have found a place on board at all, for we are actually leaving travelers behind whose applications for passage were made sixty days before yours. At this moment we have a passenger who was willing to pay six hundred dollars for a stateroom deluxe who is sleeping in the steerage, because that is the best we could do for him."

This official was assured that the brethren did not desire to be alone for selfish reasons, but only because such a thing seemed necessary for the proper completion of their work. Though understanding and appreciating their needs he was powerless to do anything for them.

Before bedtime came, however, the missionaries were alone in their own cabin. The details of how this was accomplished are unimportant and would take too long to relate here, but sitting on the side of his berth and discussing the matter, tears came into Brother McKay's eyes as he said:

"No one can tell me that things come about in this marvelous manner merely by chance. The skeptic may say the Lord has nothing to do with our arrangements, but I know He is doing for us that which we cannot do for ourselves."

This remark and the spirit which prompted it, a willingness to acknowledge the hand of the Almighty in all things, led the brethren to consider and enumerate some of the things, simple in themselves but none the less miraculous in their eyes, which had occurred during their eventful journey.

1. President Grant in setting Brother McKay apart for this work had sealed upon him the power to avoid dangers seen and unseen, together with the necessary wisdom to analyze and understand the needs of the missions which should be visited. An undeniable manifestation of this power had been received.

2. President Lund had promised Brother Cannon that if he were seasick or had any other sickness, it would be of very short duration, and though he had been a poor sailor heretofore, he was sick but five minutes, in spite of the fact that extremely rough seas had been encountered.

3. The brethren were never hindered by unfavorable weather except once, and on that occasion they were convinced the delay was for their own good. Storms which must inevitably have delayed them in their work and in some cases would have prevented their doing it, preceded them by a day or two or followed immediately after.

4. Though total strangers in the city, they were led to the best spot in Peking in which to dedicate the great Chinese realm for the preaching of the Gospel. As they became acquainted with the city subsequent to the performance of that sacred duty, they were

convinced that no place equally suitable could have been found.

5. In changing money in China, where there is so much counterfeit, they met an American at the right moment who gave them advice which was worth many dollars to them. Judging from the experience of other travelers whom they met, it was nothing short of a miracle for two men to travel as many miles as they did in China and say truthfully that they did not lose a cent in exchange or counterfeit.

6. They arrived in Shanghai at midnight, total strangers to the city and its people, and were given beds when regular customers of the hotel were being turned away. In every hotel in the city travelers were obliged to sit in the lobbies all night.

7. They secured a stateroom to themselves on a ship leaving Shanghai after the company had told them positively it could not be done.

8. This ship ran into the wharf at Kobe, Japan, and although the injury was slight it caused a delay of two days which were sufficient to enable the brethren to complete their work in that land.

9. They obtained exclusive accommodations on the vessel leaving Honolulu when to all human appearances such a thing was impossible.

10. At President Grant's suggestion, they went first to Japan. Many people thought it a very unwise itinerary, and at that time it seemed so to them. But nothing wiser could have been planned. In Japan and China the needs of those countries were seen, from the missionary point of view, and in Hawaii it was seen how some of the needs could be supplied by natives of those lands.

These and many things of a similar nature could be pointed out which the confirmed skeptic must admit were remarkable, even while denying the intervention of any higher power. But the thing worth noting is this: Such intervention DID NOT occur with other travelers. If chance were to be credited, it was showing reprehensible partiality. However, the most comforting blessing which came to these missionaries cannot be described and would not be understood by the unbeliever. That was the sweet spirit of peace and the assurance that the Lord was with them and would protect them, no matter what the outward danger was, that their loved ones would be preserved, and that every promise made them by the servant of the Lord would be fulfilled.

As the *Maui* neared the Golden Gate leading into San Francisco harbor, a fog so dense settled down upon the water that one could hardly see an object two yards away. Every few moments a bell could be heard in the distance, and guided by those sounds Captain Johnson directed the great ship, loaded with hundreds of human beings, safely to its pier. How did he do it? Because he knew the way and understood the signals.

Involuntarily the mind of the thoughtful man reverted to his Church. Did his captain know the way? Was he acquainted with the signals? Or was he, amid the darkness and fog, stubbornly ignoring every warning and blindly leading precious souls who trusted him into dangers which must inevitably overwhelm them? These travelers were devoutly thankful for the assurance they had that their captain knew the way.

Among all who are acquainted with him, President Heber J. Grant is known as an unusually big-hearted and generous man. These special missionaries had additional occasion to see and appreciate his generosity, for upon arrival in San Francisco they found he had, at his own expense, brought Sisters McKay and Cannon to California to see their husbands for two days before they should sail for the South Seas. This meeting was a joyful one, made more so by the fact that it was so entirely unexpected.

Final farewell should not be taken of Hawaii without a further word being said of the very beautiful temple which is built upon an eminence overlooking the sea and valley at Laie. A world traveler aboard the *Maui* told Brother McKay that it was the most beautiful of all the temples built by the Church, and indeed, he called it an architectural gem, and many of the passengers spoke in high praise of its artistic beauty. One man said he had driven past the building but was short of time and consequently did not go through it. He was not so well informed as a young lady, an American, who was met some years ago by Elder Levi Edgar Young and a party of our missionaries on one of the Swiss lakes. Upon hearing they were from Utah she asked,

"And did you really live among the Mormons? And were you ever able to get into their sanctum sanctorum, the Holy of Holies?"

"Yes, we have been in their temple."

"But I thought they didn't allow anyone but 'Mormons' to go in?"

"They don't," was Brother Young's reply, and the young lady lapsed into embarrassed silence.

For some time after World War I it was almost as difficult for an American to obtain permission to leave his own country as it is for a Japanese to come into it. One visit after another had to be made to the offices of the various consuls, particularly to the British who had to visa passports before the travelers could sail for New Zealand. The path between this office and that of the steamship company was pretty well worn. During one visit the consul said:

"I suppose you feel that you are between the devil and the deep sea."

"Yes, literally," was the answer, "when we are between the British consulate and the steamship company's office."

His sense of humor was keener than that of most consuls, for he added: "And of course you would not call the British consulate the deep sea."

It seemed necessary that the special missionaries send their passports to Washington for correction before they could sail, and as word reached President Grant just at this time that President Anthon H. Lund had passed to his glorious reward, it was decided that these brethren should return to Salt Lake, attend the funeral and have their papers properly prepared while they were waiting.

After a delightful visit in Utah, the missionaries again entered upon their journey, leaving Salt Lake City March 26th, 1921.

A day that is not crowded almost to overflowing with pressing matters is almost unendurable to Brother McKay, so when he learned upon arrival in San Francisco that the *Marama* would sail Tuesday instead of Monday, as had been expected, he decided to run down to Los Angeles to have a final visit with President Grant who was in that city. Brother Cannon promised to have everything in readiness upon his return Tuesday morning.

It was found, however, that application for permission to leave the United States must be made in person by the applicant, and in spite of appeals and explanations to the official in charge he remained obdurate. The British consul could not give the visas until these papers had been obtained, and the steamship company could not issue the tickets without a visa. Brother McKay's train, which should have arrived two hours before the boat sailed, was nearly an hour late, and it required some real hustling to secure the necessary papers and reach the *Marama* in time. Later he explained that it had seemed wholly impossible for him to board the train in Los Angeles at all, as it was made up entirely of Pullman cars and every berth had been sold. Some energetic work, combined with faith, on the part of himself and President Joseph W. McMurrin finally accomplished his purpose.

One of the interesting things met by the traveler going toward the equator for the first time is the number of flying fish which rise from the water as the ship approaches. So numerous are they that they appear like a beautiful silver cloud coming up out of the sea.

There is an old legend that when a vessel crosses the equator, Neptune and his followers come aboard and hold court, passing sentence of more or less severity upon all who are brought before him. In these modern times some enterprising passenger usually takes the old sea god's part. All passengers, both men and women, who are making their debut into the southern hemisphere, are warned that they had better dress in bathing suits or in old clothes, as they are likely to be considerably mussed up. The *Marama* was not slighted, for there was the flaxen-haired Neptune with trident and entire court, including his wife who, under her paint looked suspiciously like a brawny Scotchman who was constantly trying to borrow matches from someone. Our travelers with scores of others were hailed before him.

Brother McKay, in defiance of the warning, was dressed in his best suit of white, and many of the passengers expected to see some great sport. But Neptune after looking at him doubtfully for a few moments merely ordered that he appear at dinner with his hair parted in the middle.

The usual penalty was to have a thick coat of lather made up of what seemed to be salt water and flour spread on thickly with a stiff whitewash brush and scraped off with a rough wooden razor. A long tunnel had been formed by putting deck benches together so securely fastened that no amount of pressure from within would enlarge the aperture, and through this the novitiate had to crawl, while the hose with a heavy pressure of water behind it was turned on him. The fresh salt water was invigorating and delightful, but for a rotund man to crawl through a tunnel several sizes too small for him was not so agreeable, and the shouts of the crowd, while they may have accelerated his speed, did not add greatly to his enjoyment of the occasion.

There is something intensely fascinating about the tropical ocean. The indescribable blue of the water is only equaled by the blue of the heavens. The splendor of the sunsets will never be forgotten by one who has seen them. The gorgeous colors gradually fade away and are supplanted by the brilliant stars, than which nothing is more inclined to turn one's thoughts heavenward. The north star and the "dipper" have disappeared and the first stars of the southern cross are appearing above the horizon.

In one respect the passengers aboard the *Marama* set a praiseworthy example. The bar was closed and not a game of any kind was played on the Sabbath day. In the evening most of the passengers congregated in the social hall and sang hymns.

Twelve days after sailing from San Francisco, the special missionaries landed at Papeete, the chief city of the Tahitian or Society Islands, and called the Paris of the Pacific. The group is controlled by France and as a result there is a decidedly French air about the place. Most of the natives speak that language which is taught in the schools.

The low-lying coral islands barely rise above the water line and are very beautiful. They are covered with a dense growth of coconut and other tropical trees and vegetation, and their inhabitants appear to have the same delightful characteristics as the other Polynesian races.

CHAPTER 10

TAHITI

"He that goeth forth and weepeth, bearing precious seed, shall doubtless come again with rejoicing, bringing his sheaves with him."

—Psalm 126:6

Attractive as they appear to the traveler, the Society Islands offer many difficulties, some of them of a severely trying nature to the missionary. The visitors had a good opportunity to see a few of the unpleasant experiences with which our Elders have to contend. President L.H. Kennard, who was presiding there at the time of this visit, had gone out three months before to hold conferences on some of the islands and had not been heard from since. This situation alarmed Brother McKay greatly until explanation was made that it was not an unusual one.

There is no regular communication between the islands. The missionaries must travel on trading schooners which ply from one island to another at irregular intervals and must await their chance of finding a vessel which will bring them back to the starting place. Not infrequently an Elder after receiving his release is compelled to nurse his patience in a remote and isolated field for several months before he is able to find means of leaving for Mission headquarters, and the place of embarkation for home.

Upon the arrival of the *Marama* in the scenic harbor of Papeete, the special missionaries were met by Elders Melvin Strong, Grant L. Benson, George C. Nelson, and Wallace Martin. Of these four, Elders Nelson and Martin had been there four months awaiting an opportunity to go to their fields of labor and Elder Benson, though released some weeks before, had been unable to arrive in time to take the last boat and was obliged to wait a month for the next one. Elder McCullough, though released at the same time as Elder Benson, was not yet there and probably would not be for another two months.

Brother McKay was much perplexed as to the best thing to do. Nothing could be more uncertain than the date of President Kennard's return. He might be home in a few weeks or it might be several months. To visit any of the islands without him seemed a useless procedure and one which would have cost from $750.00 to $1,500 if a special boat were chartered. To go with a chance trading schooner and perhaps be gone for months was wholly impracticable in view of the program before the brethren.

It was tentatively decided, therefore, that Brother Cannon should remain until the special boat came along, which was scheduled for three weeks later, and with this vessel he should follow to New Zealand. Brother McKay, it was thought, had better go on with the *Marama* which was to proceed south on the following day.

The one thing which made the execution of this plan somewhat doubtful was the fact that the officials had taken up their passports as the brethren left the *Marama* in the evening. The following day was Sunday, and a great celebration was being held in honor of the newly arrived governor of the islands. Amid the confusion and excitement, and with all offices closed for Sunday, the prospect of obtaining passports seemed far from bright. But Brother McKay instructed Brother Cannon to obtain them, and as has already been stated, on this trip at least it was invariably possible to follow instructions.

The first official was awakened at six o'clock in the morning by Brothers Cannon and Benson. This gentleman promised to meet the brethren at the passport office at 8:30, a promise which he failed to keep. Every officer connected even remotely with the passport department was visited. All were helpless or unwilling to do anything.

Meanwhile the *Marama* was preparing to sail at five in the afternoon. Brother McKay attended Sunday School and afternoon meeting and Brother Cannon spent as much time in these gatherings as could be spared from his apparently fruitless efforts to obtain the necessary papers. Just before the afternoon meeting their troubles were explained to Brother Timmy, a prominent native Church member. He placed himself and his auto at their disposal. Brother Cannon went with him to the passport office. Two policemen were guarding the place, and to them Brother Timmy said:

"Two of my friends are here and must have their passes before the boat sails."

"But we have no right to touch the passes," was the answer.

"You show me where they are, then turn your backs, and I will be responsible to your superior officers."

The policemen pointed to a certain drawer and walked out of the room, and Brother Timmy secured both passes.

After the meeting Brother Cannon hurried to the boat to have his trunk and other belongings taken ashore, but Brother McKay discovered in an apparently accidental way, but in which the brethren acknowledged the hand of the Lord, that the boat on which Brother Cannon was expected to follow to New Zealand had been taken off that route and would not sail as had previously been scheduled. It was therefore hastily decided that the two missionaries should proceed together.

During the hour which intervened before the *Marama* was to weigh anchor the missionaries visited a schooner owned by a company of French traders. The captain of the vessel is a native Tahitian and a devoted member of the Church. The missionaries laboring in Papeete told a story, which he modestly confirmed, of a banquet held on board the ship as he was about to be given the command. The owners, in accordance with the prevailing custom, had provided liquor and tobacco in liberal quantities for the banquet, and some friends of this brother told him he would have to drink when they proposed a toast to the new captain. He replied he would not touch liquor. His friends with the best of intentions urged him to do so, saying the owners would consider it an insult if he refused and would doubtless take the command from him, but despite these appeals he remained obdurate.

When the night of the banquet came, someone proposed a toast to the new commander and all arose to drink it. It was then noticed that the captain himself had a glass of water in his hand. His employers enquired why, and he explained that drinking liquor was against his religious convictions. "Oh, well, take a cigar, and we will excuse you from drinking," was the reply.

"But I do not smoke either," said the brother and proceeded to explain the Word of Wisdom to the surprised and curious crowd.

The governor of the islands was present and congratulated the owners of the vessel on having a man of such character in charge of their ship. He continued:

"He will be a far more trustworthy captain if he observes what he calls the Word of Wisdom than he otherwise would be, and a man of that character may be relied upon for his honesty."

There are not many Church members in Papeete, but all were at the wharf to say good-bye, and it was evident they have the same sweet spirit which is so apparent among all true members of the Church of Christ. They are generous to a fault and the brethren were loaded with fruit, shells, and beads.

Though it was a relief to be out at sea again after the oppressively hot day on shore, the missionaries watched the land recede from view somewhat regretfully, for they felt that little had been accomplished during the brief visit. Still their especial mission was to see what the various fields needed and the need of this one seemed apparent: a 75-ton schooner which would enable the Elders to go to their fields without such extravagant waste of time and which with wise management might also enable the Church members to escape the traders, some of them unscrupulous, who call for their pearl shell and other products and pay just what they please for it.

As the brethren sailed away this thought came to their minds:

Neither one of them had ever met any of the missionaries laboring in Papeete and of course were wholly unacquainted with the members of the Church residing there. Suppose some man well informed as to Church doctrines and practices but not a member, learning of this proposed trip, had gone ahead and visited the islands professing to be Brother McKay. How long would it have taken the missionaries and faithful Church members to discover the imposition? Certainly not long. The Savior said, "And the sheep follow him: for they know his voice. And a stranger they will not follow, but will flee from him: for they know not the voice of strangers" (John 10:4-5).

The childlike faith of the natives of Tahiti is as nearly perfect, one is inclined to think, as faith can become in this world. An entire volume might be filled with accounts of faith-promoting incidents which have come to the attention of the missionaries. Sister Venus R. Rossiter, wife of President Ernest C. Rossiter who for a number of years was president of the Tahitian Mission and at the time this is being written is in charge of the French Mission, relates:

"On one occasion, Mohi, now a faithful native missionary, sailed with a number of his Chinese laborers from one of the islands of the group to Tahiti, the main island. He had on board a cargo of copra (dried coconut) and after the frail vessel had reached the open sea it was overtaken by a tremendous waterspout which literally picked it up and tossed it into the air. As the boat fell upside down the passengers and the cargo were cast into the sea. Being excellent swimmers all were able without difficulty to take care of themselves in the water and one by one succeeded in climbing onto the wrecked vessel. But there, though temporarily safe, they were helpless. For seven days and nights they sat there; alternating between hope and despair, they scanned the horizon with prayers that they might be rescued.

"One by one the Chinese laborers, exhausted by watching and overcome by the heat and the want of food and water, slipped off the overturned vessel into the sea. Attracted by the dead bodies, a large number of sharks surrounded the boat and waited hungrily for the next victim. With bodies pitiably swollen from the blistering sun and the salt water, it seemed useless to hope longer. But the undaunted Mohi continued to pray, and promised the Lord that if he and his family were rescued he would devote the remainder of his life to the preaching of the Gospel. On the evening of the seventh day, when hope had well nigh forsaken the stoutest of the gaunt and famished group, they saw a steamer coming directly toward them. Lifeboats were lowered and the party was saved.

"Through a translator the captain told Mohi that he had been induced, by an influence which to him was incomprehensible, to order the mate to change the usual course, going twenty miles farther to the right than he had ever done before, and this led the ship straight to the shipwrecked party.

"At the present writing twelve years have passed since this occurred, but true to his promise this dark-skinned but worthy man is still declaring the message of salvation to his fellowman. And not he alone, but his two sons who were with him at the time, Viao and Tuhiva, are likewise diligent and have ever been ready to explain the truth on every opportune occasion."

It is interesting to note that this same Viao is the captain heretofore mentioned in this chapter who could not be induced to drink liquor or smoke when the circumstances, to a weaker man, would have seemed to make such violation excusable.

Hotel de Diadime, Papeete, Tahiti

CHAPTER 11

RAROTONGA

"Some religious enthusiasts think only of the lilies of the field and forget the parable of the talents."
—Roger Babson

It was evening when the *Marama* cast anchor before the tiny village of Avarua on the island of Rarotonga, six hundred and thirty miles south of Tahiti. The tropical island, some of whose mountains reach a height of 3,000 feet, the intensely blue sea and the comparatively faded blue of the eastern sky, brilliant red, yellow, and green shades of the departed sun, and the purple reflection from adjacent hills all combined to furnish every imaginable gradation of color. It was truly a picturesque scene.

When entering harbors of the South Seas, the traveler inclines to the belief that the last one visited excels all others in beauty. Rarotonga is one of the most fertile and valuable of the Cook Group, and though considered an unusually good specimen of the volcanic order, it is surrounded by a coral reef, the dangerous nature of which is attested by remnants of two wrecks standing as grim sentinels at the harbor's entrance. In the waning light these crumbling hulks added to the romance of the place.

Immediately the *Marama* was surrounded by innumerable native canoes, barely large enough to carry one person and each equipped with an outrigger to prevent capsizing. As darkness crept over the enchanting scene, the occupants of the tiny skiffs took advantage of the ship's lights which attract flying fish thus making it much easier to catch these denizens of the tropical waters.

All through the night the work of discharging and taking on cargo continued. Naturally the freight taken aboard consisted principally of fruit, mostly oranges and bananas, and to sleep amid the prevailing noise was quite impossible, for the native laborers keep up a constant chattering and singing.

The next morning it was noticed that a large number of sharks surrounded the *Marama*. The sailors baited an immense iron hook attached to a thin but very strong rope and succeeded in catching a shark. He fought vigorously for liberty, but hook and rope held him though the water was lashed into foam by his desperate efforts to escape; and he was finally hauled onto the lower deck, and there killed by being hit over the nose with an iron bar. After he was supposed to be dead, he gave a last convulsive flop, striking Brother McKay with his tail and almost ruining a pair of white trousers.

A number of passengers welcomed the opportunity of riding around the small island in a Ford truck with seats along the sides. The road which skirts the seashore for the entire distance is about twenty miles long, and as it leads through a number of native villages, the travelers were able to see something of the people and their customs. Their living is indeed primitive. The "pareu" is the principal, indeed the sole, article of dress in almost every case. It resembles a red and white table cloth and is tied about the body and hangs to the knees. Of course no shoes or stockings are worn and as the only use the natives have for a house is to protect them from sun and rain their buildings are as primitive as their dress. Fish and fruit furnish the principal diet, and nature provides these in abundance.

In referring to the native dress, it is but fair to commend the modesty of the women, for when they heard or saw a party of strangers approaching they invariably disappeared from sight or put something over their shoulders.

It was interesting to learn that cement was used here long before the advent of the white man. Apparently all graves are of this material.

The claim formerly made by opponents of the Book of Mormon that cement is a modern discovery and reference to it in that record proves the book to be a fraud has long since been abandoned. Had it not been, this island would furnish evidence which is irrefutable.

When halfway around the island the driver stopped, climbed a coconut tree, and supplied the party with nuts. These when picked green furnish a most refreshing drink, and when ripe, as all know, the coconut is very good. More than that, under some circumstances it is perfectly delicious. The meat of the nut is grated and put through a process of beating and wringing until it looks like the richest of whipped cream and as for taste, well, like the Hawaiian volcano, it is indescribable. A banana of proper ripeness with this as a dressing is a dish not to be found outside the tropics. During this ride, in addition to coconuts and bananas, the travelers saw bread fruit, mangoes, guavas, oranges, and many other fruits which were unknown to them.

Two facts regarding the island are worthy of note, and do credit to the New Zealand government under whose protectorate it stands. One is that the use of intoxicants is forbidden; the other is that the land is apportioned among the natives in accordance with their needs and cannot be sold. It may be leased but usually the owners cultivate it. The result is prosperity and apparent peace. Apropos of the people working their own land, the following story comes to mind:

A number of years ago a hard-headed mayor of one of our Utah towns was making a speech at the laying of the cornerstone of a public building. To illustrate his remarks he attempted to quote

"He who by the plow would thrive,
Himself must hold the plow or drive."

Not being accustomed to quoting poetry, he got it:

"He who by the plow would thrive,
Must either hold the plow or drive himself."

The titter which arose reminded him that he had made a mistake. His next effort was:

"He who by the plow would thrive,
Must either drive himself or hold the plow."

This time the titter developed into a laugh.

"He who by the . . ." Here he floundered helplessly. "Hang it, friends, I can't quote poetry, but I know if you've got plowing to be done you had better do it yourself or watch the hired man pretty close."

As the party alighted from the Ford at the water's edge it was noticed how high the *Marama* stood out of the water, due to her light load. A young lady called attention to the fact and asked the reason. Her escort, with assumed seriousness, said, "Why the tide is out now; at high tide she will be all right." The answer satisfied the damsel until the smiles of the crowd caused her to realize how ridiculously gullible she had been.

Our travelers steamed away from the charming island, under a glorious full moon which shone upon them out of a northern sky as they were now well within the southern hemisphere. The southern cross, instead of the north pole or the "dipper," was now the outstanding group of stars. The brethren appreciated very much the opportunity of visiting this island for one day, but were no less thankful that they were not obliged to remain for a month or two until the next southbound boat came along.

An incident occurred between Rarotonga and New Zealand which may be fitly introduced here. One of the passengers was a handsome, well educated, widely traveled widow, an excellent musician and a brilliant conversationalist. Evidently her faith in the male sex was at low ebb, and her conception of Mormon morality not less so. In response to something she had said, Brother McKay spoke of our Church standards, saying our young men are taught to be as pure as the girls they marry. The lady was incredulous. Such a thing was well nigh unbelievable. Pointing an accusing finger at Brother McKay, she said, "But you cannot tell me you were virtuous when you married your wife!"

"Yes, madam, I was and have been ever since." Had the whole world seen him and listened to his answer, the whole world would have been convinced, as was the lady, that he spoke the truth. She sank back in her chair, astonished, speechless, but convinced.

CHAPTER 12

WELLINGTON, NEW ZEALAND: "HUI TAU"

"Give me a rub with thy nose,
And I will rub with mine.
Such salutations in this land
May seem to you divine;
But when I see before me now
Three hundred in a line,
'Tis just one rub for your nose,
Three hundred rubs for mine."
—Anonymous

Prior to Brother McKay's departure to preside over the European Mission in the fall of 1922, a social was given in his honor by the General Sunday School Board at the home of Elder Stephen L. Richards, of the Quorum of the Twelve, and his hospitable wife. Each Board member was asked to write a line or two of poetry about the honored guest, and the above verse, the author of which should remain unknown, purported to describe Brother McKay's arrival among the Maoris in New Zealand.

As for the number of noses, the writer might have multiplied the three hundred several times without exaggeration. But with the *Hangi*, as the New Zealand salutation is called, the noses are not rubbed but pressed against each other. If one attempts to rub, the other nose is likely to describe an arc about one's face. The degree of pressure indicates the esteem in which those participating hold each other, and with the special missionaries the *Hangi* was long and severe. At the same time the natives gave a sort of moan, with an inflection of pleasure when the noses met and of sorrow as the moment of parting approached.

Mention should be made, however, of several things which happened before the brethren were asked to greet the natives in the approved Maori fashion.

First of all they landed in Wellington, located on the south end of the north island, and were met by President George S. Taylor, now deceased, and Elders Graham H. Doxey, Julius V. Madsen, and other missionaries.

Here in the steamship company's storeroom, Brother McKay found his trunk, just as he said he would, though it had been unaccountably lost in San Francisco when the travelers arrived from Hawaii. How it came to be sent to this far-off land will ever remain a mystery.

While in Wellington, the capital of New Zealand, a call was made on Dr. Pomare, one of the colonial ministers and a highly educated gentleman, who had made a study of the effect of Mormonism upon the Maoris. The doctor himself has some native blood in his veins and is proud of the fact, as well he might be. He made the positive statement in answer to a question by Brother McKay, that he wished all the natives were Mormons, for then, "They would all be decent citizens." Since this visit was made, Dr. Pomare has been knighted by the king of England.

The great annual event among Church members in New Zealand is the "Hui Tau," or mission conference, which is held during the autumn month of April. Followers of this narrative will understand they are now in the southern hemisphere where there is a complete reversal of seasons. Christmas comes almost in midsummer.

Many of the Maoris are comparatively wealthy, and they have purchased a number of immense tents, comparable in size to those used by a three-ringed circus in the United States. One of the largest of these is used for meetings and at night as an immense bedroom, the beds being made upon the ground. Brother McKay has described it thus: "Every four feet around its entire circumference constituted a bedroom, and a similar double tier extended from the speaker's stand down the middle to the opposite end. Thus feet to feet hundreds of heads pointed toward the outside and hundreds of others toward the middle of the tent, a passageway being left open all around this combination bedroom and assembly hall; beds remaining intact, and were sat upon or reclined upon during the services.

"For the convenience of those people who like to sleep in Church, I recommend this combination scheme most highly."

The "Hui Tau" of 1921, the year of the visit herein described, was held in the outskirts of Huntly, a village of the Waikato district in the "heart of Maoriland." On the train en route to this place the visitors met a number of Church members who were going to the conference and were introduced to them and to the *Hangi* at the same time; and although the missionaries felt that their noses were pressed quite out of shape, this was but a foretaste of that which was to come.

A prominent figure of the gathering was Sid Christy, who now holds the title of chief among his people. For some years he was in Salt Lake, a student of the Latter-day Saints High School and a star on the basketball team. He is now married and has a large family. Speaking of the *Hangi* and comparing it with the white people's habit of kissing, he thought the advantages were all in favor of the native custom. He said, "If you kiss a man's wife, he is likely to beat you up, but the *Hangi* which means the same thing to us, can be indulged in with impunity."

The tents were erected in a vacant field about a mile outside the city limits and all roads seemed to lead to the place, for in every direction one could see crowds on foot and in vehicles of various kinds pressing thither. Again we quote from Brother McKay:

"Hundreds of people were already assembled in the open space between us and the two largest tents; and what we saw and participated in during the next two hours contributed to make that day one of the most unique and interesting of this extensive tour.

"Sister Taylor, Miss Miriam, and others from the Mission House had joined us. Brother Sid Christy had come bounding to extend greetings and fortunately for us, put us at our ease by timely suggestions and explanations. As our party began to walk slowly toward the assembled multitude, our ears were greeted by a shrill cry from a score of women's voices, 'Haere Mai! Haere Mai!' and other terms of welcome, accompanied by such wild gesticulations, jumping, dancing and grimacing that, had it not been for the assurances of Brother Christy, I should have thought we were about to be attacked instead of welcomed.

"This welcome was followed by the 'Haka' or war dance by a dozen men or more in front of the crowd, urged enticingly on by the dancing of two women, one at each end of the row of warriors. How they wriggled and writhed, rolling their eyes until only the whites were visible, lolled their tongues and made unsightly grimaces! I was fascinated and yet worried because surely some acknowledgment must be made of this most demonstrative welcome.

"However, when within a hundred yards of the dancing group, we were told to stand still. The representative of the 'king' of the district, an uncle, we were informed, stepped forward, flourishing a cane, and walking briskly forward and back, delivered an impassioned address of welcome. He was followed by the next man in rank, and he by several others, each expressing his joy and gratitude for the visit of those who had traveled so far to meet them.

"At this point we should have followed in true Maori fashion, but as the crowd was waiting to shake our hands, it was suggested by our host that they would 'accept the *Hangi* as a gracious reply.' And so, beginning with the woman on our left, we clasped hands and pressed noses with the entire assembly!

"Again we learned by experience that the *Hangi* varies in degree and intensity as does our kiss, though perhaps not with the same significance.

"As we took our places in the seats provided for us, we saw entering the grounds a group of visiting Maoris.

"'Haere Mai! Haere Mai!' again cried the women, and again the gesticulating, dancing and speech making.

"Then we saw the reciprocal performance. At the conclusion of the addresses as mentioned above, both sides remained silent, and all heads were bowed. Soon we heard moans, and we noticed that men and women were crying. It was not make-believe, either, for tears were flowing. This was the *Tangi* part of the welcome. They were expressing sympathy for those who had lost loved ones during the past year. Following this, the leading man among the visitors, flourishing his cane, responded to the welcome, and told why they had come. He was followed by others, and then the group retired to give place for other groups to follow. Thus the home people welcome the visitors all through the day!

"The next morning we received evidence, and each succeeding day confirmation, that the 'Hui Tau' is a well disciplined organization. Every person on the grounds was expected to respond with promptness and dispatch to the following signals:

"At 6:15 a.m. a clanging bell drove Morpheus to his sunless cave and bade his subjects get up!

"At 7 a.m. it called to 'Karakia' or morning service; at 8 a.m. to 'Kai' (breakfast); at 10 a.m. to 'Karakia' or first session of conference; 1 p.m. to 'Kai' (lunch); 2 p.m. to 'Karakia,' second session of conference; 5 p.m. to 'Kai' (dinner); 6:30 p.m. to 'Karakia,' evening service; 7 p.m. to the evening session of the conference.

"Twice a day as intimated above, everybody excepting the women folk preparing the breakfast, assembled in the large tent and participated in devotional services consisting of (1) singing, (2) prayer, (3) repeating in concert passages of scripture, and (4) questions and discussion. The quotations were selected from the Ready References, and chanted in unison. It was significant that only the older Maoris participated in this memory work, the younger ones who joined them read from the book. This is explained by the fact that when the Gospel first came among the Maoris, very few could read, so they memorized what was taught them. The chant or song was given as an aid to memory. There were those present who can repeat every passage in the Ready References, under its appropriate subject. The meaning of the passages was made clear, and their applicability to the latter-day work shown during the discussion that followed. It was plainly evident that the Maoris had assembled to learn more of the Gospel of Christ, and not merely to be entertained.

"Following the service, as many as could be seated at the first tables, answered the call to 'Kai.' Under a canopy fully as large as that in which services were held, were arranged eight long tables each with a seating capacity of forty persons. Four girls furnished these tables and served the guests, each group taking charge of eighty persons at every sitting.

"Each group, too, had its own boiler for cooking, its own tanks for dish-washing and its own cupboards for the dishes, and every plate, cup and saucer, knife, fork and spoon was accounted for.

"Boiled meat, potatoes, spinach, bread, butter, jam and cheese made the principal eatables; but cake, watermelons, and other fruits and delicacies were also served. Some of the meat and potatoes were prepared in the 'Hangi,' that is, cooked in a pit in the good old Maori fashion, except that chains were heated instead of rocks. And we must admit that meat thus cooked is far more tender and delicious than that boiled in the more modern manner.

"As the women peeled the potatoes, it seemed by the ton, or washed dishes, literally by the hundred, they worked in unison to the rhythm of some song, hummed as gleefully as though they were having a Jubilee. Sometimes the young girls having 'finished the dishes' would wind up with a touch of the 'Kopi Kopi' or 'Hula Hula.'

"How efficient this organization and how effectively it worked may be partly realized when I tell you that during the four and one half days of the 'Hui Tau' approximately 10,000 meals were served! And that, too, without any apparent extraordinary effort!

"Some of the best homes in the district were given over entirely to the accommodation of the visitors, Elder Cannon and I each having a room and a bed as comfortable as one could wish. The fifty Elders, however, did not fare so well. They slept on mats laid on straw on the floor of the Church. It was truly a community bedroom!

"While the religious purpose of the 'Hui Tau' is evident on every hand, and Gospel conversations and discussions are carried on with almost every group between meetings, there is no dearth of amusement and legitimate entertainment. Chief among these I think I shall name the 'Poi Dance' as given on two different occasions by fifteen young Maori maidens dressed in native costume. Combining as it does rhythm, beauty, grace and skill, the 'Poi Dance' easily ranks among the most beautiful dances of the world. I have never seen any that excel it.

"If the 'Poi' is beautiful, the 'Haka' is the most thrilling! After seeing this native war dance, one can readily understand how the ancient warriors, aroused to the highest pitch of enthusiasm, if not frenzy, rushed so madly into battle, or stormed with bare hands and naked bodies almost impregnable 'pas!'

"We were given a glimpse, too, of the 'Koro Phio Pi' or 'Hula Hula,' but one of the native brethren suggested that they 'go slow on that,' and 'a hint to the wise' was in this case 'sufficient.'

"Too much credit cannot be given to the 'Hui Tau' committee, composed entirely of native men, who have so successfully managed these gatherings for many years. Brother William Duncan is chairman and a more able, loyal Church worker than he is seldom found anywhere in the world! He is a man among men, a worthy example of what 'Mormonism' will do for those who will accept and live it! He has been ably assisted by four others, equally worthy of commendation and esteem.

"Though each annual gathering costs between $2,500 and $3,000, the committee is free from debt and has a fair balance in the bank. Besides this, they have accumulated considerable property, such as tents, a dynamo, electrical appliances, stoves etc., etc.

"But the things mentioned above are only adjuncts to the principal features of this notable gathering! The glory of the 'Hui Tau' is seen and felt in the twelve or fourteen worshiping assemblies which culminated in a wonderfully inspirational priesthood meeting. The earnestness, faith and devotion of the audience, the manifestation of the inspiration of the Lord upon the speakers, native as well as European, the excellent music, and the confidence, sympathy, and brotherly love that flowed from soul to soul, all combined to make every service a supreme joy.

"Not the least remarkable feature of this memorable event was the skill, the intelligence, the accuracy, and the inspiration with which Elder Stewart Meha interpreted the addresses of the visiting brethren. His interpretation was simply marvelous! Truly he was remarkably blessed. [See also INTERPRETATION OF TONGUES—Appendix B.]

"The spirit, intelligence, and earnestness of the three score elders and lady missionaries were distinct contributions to the success of each session. No more devoted self-sacrificing men and women can be found anywhere in the world. I could not help but think how proud and happy the parents and wives of those young men would be if they could have seen these missionaries in the glory of their work as we met them!

"Success and long life to the 'Hui Tau'! May each succeeding one be more successful than the last! May its influence extend until it becomes a power not only to cement the love and increase the faith of the Church members, as it does even now, but also to break down the barriers erected by the ignorant and vicious to impede the progress of the Church of Christ."

The lady missionaries referred to by Brother McKay were Ida A. Taylor, wife of President George S. Taylor, Austin Schwendiman, wife of Mission Secretary Frederick W. Schwendiman, Ida F. Stott, wife of Principal Franklin E. Stott of the Church Agricultural College, Flora D. Fisher, wife of Elder Fisher, a teacher in the College, and Sisters Miriam and Priscilla Taylor, daughters of the Mission President.

The district in which the "Hui Tau" is held furnishes the food, which is served without cost, and all on the grounds are welcome, regardless of whether or not they are affiliated with the Church. On this occasion fourteen beeves and thirty sheep were contributed by prosperous farmers and much more meat was purchased from butchers. Potatoes and vegetables came in by the wagon load and large sums were contributed in cash. The efforts made by Church members and non-members to secure this gathering for their district on the following year impress one with the thought that contributions are gladly given.

Before this chapter is closed credit should be given to Elders Gordon C. Young and Roland C. Parry, both of whom speak the Maori language fluently, for the assistance they gave the visitors in translating for their benefit the sermons and remarks of the native brethren.

Crowd in Hui Tau Tent, New Zealand

Native Crowd, New Zealand

Hui Tau Tents

CHAPTER 13

MAORIS, FIJI, AND TONGA QUARANTINE

"Prayer prevents sin, and sin prevents prayer."
—Brigham Young

Had doubt existed as to the wisdom of having one of the Twelve visit outlying missions, it would have been entirely dispelled during the "Hui Tau." Brother McKay preached the Gospel with the power of his holy calling upon him, as indeed he had done in all lands previously visited. Missionaries and Saints listened raptly to his inspired words. They had anticipated his coming with joy and were in nowise disappointed with message or messenger. Maoris and whites alike will always hold him in loving remembrance. His sermons were of a nature to awaken, not merely a temporary enthusiasm which would pass when farewell was said, but a deep and abiding love for the truth.

More than one was heard to express devout gratitude for the testimony, divinely given, that "he gave some, apostles; and some prophets . . . for the perfecting of the saints, for the work of the ministry, for the edifying of the body of Christ: till we all come in the unity of the faith, and of the knowledge of the Son of God, unto a perfect man, unto the measure of the stature of the fulness of Christ" (Ephesians 4:11-13).

Even strangers who attended the meetings out of curiosity—for many came from Auckland and other places drawn by the news that an Apostle from Utah was among them—were deeply impressed. The words of St. Matthew might well be quoted to describe this visit: "The people were astonished at his doctrine: for he taught them as one having authority, and not as the scribes" (Matthew 7:28-29).

Many persons afflicted with disease were blessed during the conference, and before its completion testified that they were much improved in health. One woman who had been married for several years and had prayed for a child was promised that her prayers should be answered. Shortly after their return home the brethren learned that this prediction had been fulfilled.

In the missionary meeting many splendid testimonies were borne, all of which were worthy of being recorded. One alone must suffice. Elder Halvey E. Bachman said his prayer had been that he might fill a mission, but nine years previous to this time he was afflicted with enlargement of the heart and his doctor had stated he would never be able to leave his bed. Brother Jonathan G. Kimball promised him he would fill a mission and in a patriarchal blessing this promise was repeated.

It might be added that these prophecies were literally fulfilled. He completed his labors in New Zealand, received an honorable release and has since died.

The Maoris, with all other Polynesians who have accepted the Gospel, love it sincerely and furnish splendid evidence of its power to save. They understand that salvation comes through obedience to law, and these humble people manifest a childlike obedience. They naturally love to smoke, drink, and gamble, but in almost every case these weaknesses are laid aside when they begin seriously to investigate the principles of truth. They comprehend better than some highly civilized nations that the Gospel redeems men from sin but cannot save them in sin.

The ability to sincerely repent is also a native characteristic. When a Maori falls into wrongdoing whether the offense be trivial or serious, he usually comes to the proper officers, makes confession, and humbly seeks forgiveness. Men who have been guilty of violating the Word of Wisdom often refuse to open a meeting with prayer or perform any other duty.

A typical example of this characteristic was called to the attention of the visitors. In a branch which during the world war had been left alone because of shortage of missionaries, one of the native brethren had returned to his former habit of smoking. Elder Graham H. Doxey, now Bishop of the Third Ward in Salt Lake City, and a companion were sent to this branch to learn conditions. The brother was asked to open meeting with prayer, but to the surprise of the missionaries he declined to do so. They afterwards asked why, when he held the priesthood and at one time had been very active.

"I have been guilty of smoking," the man answered penitently. "The other members know it, and I could not face them if I addressed the Lord in their presence when I have not been keeping His law."

Mingling with the members of the Church at the "Hui Tau" were two missionaries of the Reorganized Church who did their utmost to attract attention. More than one meeting was disturbed by the questions which they shouted at the speaker. Whenever they could find anyone who would listen, they followed their usual custom and berated the Utah Mormons in a shameful manner. Finally they became so abusive that Elder Benjamin Brown and two local brethren told them they must conduct themselves as gentlemen or leave the place.

Apparently they had no desire to do either, and at last the brethren decided that patience had ceased to be a virtue. A young Maori, a star player on the Church school football team, lifted the more obstreperous of the two offenders over the fence, and the other undesirable visitor beat the athlete to the gate by a few inches. It is worthy of note that these two men had partaken of the food which was dispensed without charge in the dining tent.

Subsequently the three brethren who had taken matters into their own hands were summoned before Brother McKay. They approached him with considerable trepidation, uncertain how he would view their action.

"Did you throw that man over the fence?" he sternly asked the young native.

"Yes, sir, but I . . . but he . . ."

There was no occasion to finish, for Brother McKay took him in his arms and gave him a hug which brought peace to his heart and a smile to his face which did not disappear as long as the conference lasted.

It is a delight to mingle with the Maoris. Men six feet tall and over were greatly in evidence, and there was a dignity—something even king-like—about them which was most admirable.

Generosity appears to be a racial trait. To illustrate this: Elder Elmo F. Jacobs had just received word of his father's death, and he was released to assume the responsibility of caring for his mother and six younger children. A purse containing $175 was raised for him in a few moments and at the same time $200 was collected to pay the balance on a meetinghouse which had been erected in one of the branches. Nor did it end there. Elder Rulon N. Manning had the misfortune to lose his pocketbook with $25 in it. This amount, and a little more, was handed him.

The visiting brethren also have occasion to remember this generous spirit. While at the home of Brother William Duncan, already referred to in a former chapter, he presented each of them with a beautiful and costly traveling rug. These gifts were modestly given in the name of the "Hui Tau" committee. But when asked for the names and addresses of the members who had contributed, so that letters of thanks could be sent them, he hesitated. Brother McKay insisted.

"But they don't know the rugs are being given," Brother Duncan stammered.

Further questioning revealed the fact that he was presenting the rugs personally but was trying to give the committee credit for the kind act.

In the beautiful home of this faithful native brother there is a room which is kept exclusively for use of the mission president when he visits this part of his field, in addition to which there are always accommodations for all the Elders who travel that way.

The difficulties encountered in the Orient in securing places on steamers were repeated here. Only after considerable difficulty were the brethren able to find anything on the *Tofua*, which was sailing for the Tongan and Samoan Islands. It was not necessary to say good-bye to New Zealand or to its interesting people, for they were to return and finish their work here after making a tour of the missions on the islands above mentioned.

In the first chapter of this work, reference was made to a cabin which was assigned to our missionaries and two priests. During the five days that the four were together many pleasant conversations were had, in which the Catholics, at least the one who was not bedfast from seasickness, asked many questions about Church organization and policy. Particularly was he interested in our missionary system. He seemed fair-minded and was certainly courteous and highly educated.

The entrance to the harbor of Suva, principal city of the Fiji group, is a devious one. The vessel winds in and out in order to avoid the dangerous but attractive reef. The water swarmed with sharks.

Here was another new world. No hats are worn either by native men or women, great bushy heads of hair protecting them from the intense tropical heat. Naturally shoes and stockings are never worn, and the dress of the men consists merely of a "lavalava," a cloth tied about the loins and hanging to the knees. The women are somewhat more modestly attired.

The Fijians seem to be inordinately fond of jewelry. Not alone the women, but men and boys also wear earrings and many of them nose rings. Frequently a button, apparently of gold, is fastened through the side of the nose and not infrequently there is one on each side as well as a pendant hanging from the nose over the upper lip. One woman was seen who had cut the lobes of her ears until they hung down in long and disgusting rings.

Though scarcely a generation has passed since these people were cannibals they appear to be good-natured and kindly. Unlike the Polynesians, they are of the Negroid race and closely resemble the negroes of our own land in general type. They are like the American colored folks, too, in this, that when religion does strike them, they manifest it in a fervent and ostentatious manner. As yet no missionary work has been done among them by this Church.

No human painter has ever been able to adequately reproduce the richness of coloring which one sees in sky and water of the South Seas. How could they when these colors were put together by the greatest of all Masters! Beautiful as is the harbor of Suva, that of Nukualofa, capital of the Tongan or Friendly Islands, surpassed it. This is rated by globe-trotters as being one of the most scenic of the world. Here, too, a skillful navigator is required to direct the vessel's course so that she will avoid the numerous small islands and coral reefs among which she must wind, making an immense letter S before reaching the point of anchorage.

Our travelers had heard so much of the harbors of this group that they feared their expectations were too high to ever be realized, but after seeing them they felt "the half has never been told." First of all as they drew near the reef, there was the ghostly wreck of the steamer *Knight of St. George,* standing high on the rocks, a monument to the folly of a captain who thought he could run a ship and drink liquor at the same time. She has already been there ten years and was gradually succumbing to waves, storms, and rust.

One could look through the clear water whose hues were as variable as that of a chameleon, and often the bottom of the ocean could be seen, with the coral formation which is being built up, so that at some future period of time the land will extend much farther seaward than at present. A long, low island in the distance resembled a man of war, the tall, slender coconut palms being the masts.

The highest point on the main island, Tongatabu on which Nukualofa is situated, is ninety feet so that the climate is even more equable than that of Samoa or Fiji.

Much to their disappointment, the special missionaries were not allowed to go beyond the wharf, as the ship and consequently the passengers, were quarantined because of an epidemic of measles which had prevailed in Fiji. As this is a much dreaded disease among the natives the officials were determined to run no risks.

President Mark V. Coombs, of the Tongan Mission, and Elder J. Kenneth Rallison, who was released to return home, came aboard the *Tofua* and proceeded with the brethren to Samoa, where President Coombs had labored as a missionary in former years.

Not a whit behind the harbor of Nukualofa in scenic beauty was that of Neiafu, the chief city of the Vavau group, a part of the Friendly Islands.

Though they had little reason to expect visitors, Elder Stirling I. May and Elder Reuben Wiberg of the last named place were at the wharf, or at least as near it as quarantine regulations permitted them to come. In an incredibly short time they had their native brass band together and much to the delight of the ship's passengers played some stirring selections. The officials apparently thought that if the measles germs were strained through a picket fence, no serious danger would ensue and the visitors were able to speak to the assembled members through an interpreter—and through the fence. Incidentally, a number of their fellow voyagers, with whom the brethren shared the loads of fruit and coconuts which had been brought them, heard something of the Gospel; and this resulted in many questions being asked subsequently.

After a few hours spent here, the *Tofua*, which had come winding into the harbor, began the process of unwinding to reach the open sea. Before this was reached, however, the ship dropped anchor and in two immense lifeboats, holding about fifty people each, the passengers who cared to go were taken to the famed "Swallows' Cave." This is located in the tiny mountain island of Otea. The cave is sufficiently large that it was possible to row both boats into the great opening at the same time and several others might have accompanied them without overcrowding. The water in the cavern is most changeable in color, inky blue, almost purple, and every variety of green. Stalactites, with many colored surfaces and of varied and grotesque forms, hung from the roof. Crabs ran or crawled along the sides, sparrows flew about screaming protestations against this violation of their sanctuary.

President Cannon in Gardens, Suva, Fiji

CHAPTER 14

WESTERN SAMOA

"No man can become a saint in his sleep."
—Henry Drummond

Anent the scant clothing worn by natives of the South Seas, Elder Ralliston relates the story of a belated Tongan passenger who rushed frantically to the wharf just as the steamer was leaving. Not wishing to draw up to the pier again, the sailors who had been using the derrick to unload freight swung it around and told him to take hold of the rope with which they would bring him to the deck where a large number of passengers were congregated. With the man hanging high in the air and his lavalava fluttering in the stiff breeze the men, deciding to have a little amusement, began swinging him about. Clinging desperately to the rope he first dropped the bundle from under his arm, then a look of horror crept over his face for the lavalava had begun to loosen. He clutched at it convulsively with one hand, but his hold on the swinging rope was uncertain, and it became a question of losing his sole covering or falling himself to the deck or perhaps into the water. He chose the first alternative and hung grimly on with both hands and thus unadorned was lowered to the vessel to the great amusement of the male and the consternation and instant dispersion of female passengers.

The Samoan or Navigator Islands lie near that mythical line, the 180th meridian, where an eastbound ship "sails out of one day into the day before." Or if the direction be westward, it sails out of today into day after tomorrow. To illustrate: The *Tofua* anchored in Apia roadstead, having come from the west, Wednesday evening. The special missionaries slept on board all night and it was still Wednesday morning when they landed. After their visit was completed, they sailed away from Apia going toward the west on Monday evening; the next morning when they arose it was Wednesday.

Not only are South Sea scenes exquisitely beautiful, but there is about them a subtle power which makes one forget previous experiences and sincerely feel that the present excels in charm everything heretofore seen. So thought the brethren while steaming between the islands of Savaii and Upolu as they approached Apia. The sun had set, leaving behind it the usual gorgeous tropical tints. Not even a ripple disturbed the mirror-like surface of the sea. Above Savaii were heavy dark clouds casting shadows of nameless color over land and water, and the crescent moon gave a finishing touch to this scene of romance and beauty.

But why attempt to describe the indescribable! As Brother McKay said, "These scrubby words are so lifeless in comparison that they make a beautiful South Sea twilight look like an American sign board."

It is not possible for large vessels to draw up to the pier at Apia, owing to the shallowness of the water. The *Tofua*, therefore, anchored out in the crescent shaped harbor and was immediately surrounded by boats. In one of these President John Q. Adams and Elders Gilbert R. Tingey, George W. Robinson, Walter J. Phillips, Cleon J. Wilcox, and Chauncey L. Witbeck were seated. They reported that preparations had been made to welcome the visitors, but owing to the late hour their program could be carried out better in the morning. Brother McKay acquiesced and another night was spent onboard.

The welcome accorded the visitors is quite as indescribable as a tropical landscape or sunset. President Adams and his wife, Thurza T. Adams, and Elder Frank D. Griffiths and his wife, Retta M. Griffiths, were early alongside the *Tofua*, each couple being in a long rowboat decorated with garlands of vines and flowers. Brother McKay was taken in one of these boats with twenty-two muscular and highly elated natives handling the usual long oars. Brother Cannon and President Coombs were taken in the other with Brother and Sister Griffiths and eighteen sturdy rowers who used short paddles instead of oars; and when they applied their strength in perfect unison to these paddles the boat almost jumped out from under its occupants. The boys had to be held in check as they were much inclined to beat the boat with the chief visitor to the pier.

Upon landing, the custom officials threw open the gates and courteously declined to make any examination of luggage. The streets were packed with people, and the Church school band from Sauniatu, composed of native boys with the exception of Elder Ray W. Berrett, played stirring strains. After the greetings were over, a procession was formed headed by the band, and the visitors were taken to Mission headquarters. Business in the town was at a standstill. Stores, banks, and offices were closed and everybody was on the streets. All had heard of Apostles, but this was the first opportunity ever given most of these people to see one. Be it said to the credit of practically all the natives and a large percentage of whites, that regardless of their own religious beliefs they looked upon Brother McKay as a divinely called servant of the Lord.

As the procession passed the school, the children and their teachers were standing at attention in front of the building and among them were the priests who from Auckland to Fiji had occupied the same cabin with the brethren. The pleasant greeting which they extended as the procession passed indicated that the association had given them a better understanding of the Church and its representatives.

It is estimated that at least fifteen hundred people were assembled on the spacious grounds of the Mission Home. Among them were the ex-king, Malietoa and his wife, U.S. Consul Quincy Roberts and his wife Dr. Roberts, the Chinese consul and two score or more of high chiefs of the islands, many of them Church members but also a number who were not. Under a large bowery erected especially for the occasion about three hundred people sat down, cross-legged, to partake of a feast, the excellence of which could hardly be surpassed in any land.

Chapters might be written on the details of this highly interesting welcome but to go into detail would prolong the narrative far beyond reasonable length. Reference must be made, however, to the visits made by tribes from surrounding villages who came scantily clad but in organized and well disciplined bodies. At the head of each group were two maids honored with this position because of their virtue. These groups looked very warlike, but there was nothing but kindness and a desire to show courtesy in their acts. All were loaded with presents of mats and beads, fans and rings of shell and silver, for the guests. Before the ceremonies were concluded there were great piles of these gifts, many of which were very rare and precious.

Then came the highest honor which can be shown a visitor, the drinking of "Kava" with the chiefs of the various tribes. No council, howsoever dignified its members nor how important the matters before it for consideration, could excel this august gathering in solemnity. No one who has been present on a similar occasion is likely to easily forget it. One could not withhold admiration for these kingly men, though their clothing consisted merely of the lavalava and shirt and they were sitting on the floor cross-legged.

Here the virgin who has been specially chosen to occupy the most exalted position among her sex prepares the drink which is made from the root of the kava. The juice from this root is now extracted by beating it to a pulp. Formerly the dusky maid chewed it and spit the juice into the wooden receptacle, but in the interest of sanitation that method has been abandoned, for which Brother McKay was duly thankful. During its preparation a discussion occurs among the chiefs as to who is to be honored with the presidency of the gathering. In this instance each deferred to the other, but finally that question was settled, and the chief selected for the place made the following speech which was translated and written by President Adams:

"This is a blessed day. It is as a fragrant and beauteous flower.

The spirit of love prevails. No wonder, as has been said, a certain Gardener was highly pleased when he visited his garden and found it filled with fragrance from many different flowers. In delight he ordered the wind to blow to all parts of the world bearing this sweetness. Such an instance is to be compared to this blessed day on which we meet. Our hearts are filled with joy and thankfulness to the Almighty King for permitting us to meet on this memorable occasion. Solomon said 'Hope deferred maketh the heart sick; but when the desire cometh it is a Tree of Life.'

"We welcome you, Apostle McKay and President Cannon, and it is a pleasure to meet you in these Samoan Islands. Thankful are we to heaven that your trip was a pleasant one and that we who awaited your coming have been blessed. Let us love, not alone with words and lips, but with hearts and action.

"This is a little tribute, Brothers McKay and Cannon, we would like to give you so you may realize that we appreciate seeing you. May your Excellencies and this people whom you are visiting be blessed."

After a suitable response from Brother McKay, other chiefs spoke, and then the question was put: "Who is the greatest chief among us and to whom shall we give the first cup of kava?" The answer was unanimous:

"Apostolo McKay," and one of the men received the cup from the maiden and with a sweeping bow presented it to their guest. After this the others, according to their rank, were served.

Sitting cross-legged for two hours is not a feat to be lightly undertaken and the only thing which detracted from the solemnity and interest of this occasion was the fact that the visitors' limbs became so cramped as to awaken a tormenting fear that these useful appendages would be useless ever afterwards.

All Polynesians seem to be alike in the matter of generosity. It is said that all food for the feasts and $400 in cash were contributed by Church members and friends, not an inconsiderable part coming from the latter class.

But it may be said here as it was said of the New Zealand gathering, that its main purpose was not to eat and sing and visit one with another. Very early the next morning, and without the use of a spade, shovel, hammer, nail, rope, or string, a very excellent bowery was erected in which to hold meetings, it being evident the regular chapel was entirely too small for the occasion. The sides of the building were open and the roof was composed of banana and palm leaves laid upon a framework of poles. It was sufficient to keep out the scorching rays of the sun and also a moderate shower of rain.

Under this shelter a crowd of eager people gathered. Chairs were furnished for the visitors and for presiding brethren and sisters; all others sat Samoan fashion on mats which they had brought with them.

One of the interesting features of these and other meetings held in this land is that when the speaker refers to a passage of scripture, there is a keen race to see who among the congregation can find it first, the winner reading it aloud.

Here, as in other missions visited, Brother McKay preached Christ and him crucified and the restored Gospel in a manner which will never be forgotten by his hearers.

In a meeting held with the missionaries, local brethren as well as Elders from Utah, almost every man who reported said the people were anxious to have their children taught the Word of Wisdom, whether they themselves belonged to the Church or observed this commandment or not, for they acknowledged it as the best doctrine ever brought to the islands.

Between meetings, chiefs from distant as well as nearby tribes visited the grounds, brought gifts, made speeches, bore testimony to the good the Church is doing, and promised to assist with the commendable work. President Adams stated that the participation of outside chiefs in this welcome and the resultant removal of prejudice would justify the world trip, even had nothing else been accomplished.

During this conference an unusually impressive baptism service was held in a limpid stream near the Mission Home. Amid tropical foliage and surrounded by the white-clad figures, those present felt they were standing almost in the visible presence of angels. Elder

Ralph A. Thacker led twenty-one humble converts into the water, among them was Robert Reid, said to be the most influential half-caste in British Samoa. Brother Reid's father was a dear friend of Robert Louis Stevenson who, as is well known, lived for a long time on these islands and whose body lies buried on a nearby hillside. This young man was named after the author.

Missionaries laboring in this field were equal in integrity to those found elsewhere in the world. From President Adams down there was not a man who would not willingly have given his life for the work if that had been required. Among these faithful workers were two young fellows, Gilbert R. Tingey and Clarence Henderson, both orphans, who were preaching the Gospel on their own means.

And it is hardly necessary to say that the sisters were not one whit behind in the matter of devotion. Indeed, the visitors had occasion to marvel at the unselfish willingness to sacrifice themselves and their own comfort which was manifested by the good women in every field visited. Sister Adams is a gem of rare quality, and this might truly be said of all the wives of mission presidents and indeed, of all lady missionaries.

Nor are the heroines of Mormondom all in the mission field. Several of the Elders had widowed mothers who were obliged to struggle exceedingly hard to support their sons. What a blessing to the Church these women are! The writer of these lines is acquainted with a sister whose two sons were laboring in Europe. She and her husband received a letter from the mission president stating that the boys were doing excellent work. At the time this word was received the mother was tired, perhaps somewhat discouraged with the extra burden that was placed upon her through lack of their help, but she sat down and cried for pure joy. Yes, she cried out of sheer happiness, although the world would hardly understand how a woman could cry for joy just because she and her husband had to send $75 or $80 away each month for the boys' support and at the same time be deprived of their assistance and companionship.

Another devoted mother, also with two sons in the field, was called, after a painful and expensive sickness, to her final reward. Her husband was in straitened financial circumstances and himself had very poor health, but the dying woman's last words were, "My boys must remain at their posts and finish their missions." The mother in this case belonged to the fourth generation in the Church and her husband to the third.

Boat, Samoa

Elder David O. McKay & President Hugh J. Cannon, Apia, Samoa

Baptism in the Rain, Apia, Samoa

CHAPTER 15

AMERICAN SAMOA

"When heaven sends trouble, there is always a means of sustaining it, but a man's own folly is a thing from which he rarely escapes."

—Tia-Kia, ancient Chinese king

All travelers who enter the harbor of Apia, capital of Western Samoa, soon hear of the disaster of March 15th and 16th, 1889. If unfamiliar with the story they solicit a recital of it upon seeing the huge mass of rusting steel which has lain on the reef for nearly two score years, but which still bears the outlines of a ship.

A terse but graphic account of the frightful hurricane which caused this wreck is found in the Samoan Mission history written by Elder Joseph H. Dean, at that time Mission president. On the date mentioned, seven battleships were anchored in the roadstead some little distance out from the pier at Apia. They were the British *Calliope*, the American *Trenton*, *Vandalia*, and *Nipsic*; and the German *Olga*, *Adler*, and *Eber*.

President Dean and Elders A. Beesley and Edward J. Wood, all well known to Church people, had come in a small boat to Apia from the island of Tutuila and were eyewitnesses to much of the disaster herein imperfectly described. On the way over their little craft was capsized, the baggage had gone to the bottom, and they narrowly escaped drowning. Their lives were saved by natives who subsequently plunged into the water and recovered the lost satchels. While preparing to return to Tutuila they were strongly prompted not to do so. Had this warning been ignored they must inevitably have perished in the appalling storm which arose when they would have been well out at sea. Surely guardian angels watch over missionaries.

The storm began Friday, March 15th. Riding idly at anchor, the war vessels were unable to obtain full head of steam before the hurricane in all its devastating fury broke upon them. Shortly thereafter the *Eber* and the *Adler* were driven onto the coral reef with such force that they were torn almost to pieces, and one hundred of their men were drowned or beaten to death on the rocks.

Through the long night the officers and men aboard the vessels worked like demons in an effort to reach the open sea where there was at least a measure of safety, but in spite of their maneuvers, with bows pointed seaward, with full steam on and all anchors down they could not withstand the gale and were being slowly driven toward the rocks and certain destruction.

Trees were laid low, houses were demolished and the roar of the breakers resembled the thunder of a thousand cannons.

Saturday morning came, and, convinced that his ship was doomed and hoping that the hundreds of natives might be able to save at least a part of his crew, the *Nipsic's* captain deliberately drew up anchors, turned the bow landward and with full steam ahead, and the hurricane helping him on, drove her as high onto the rocks as possible. His vessel was of course wrecked, but the natives responded most heroically. Repeatedly they dashed into the surf with a lifeline, only to be dragged back beaten into unconsciousness by the tremendous waves. Finally one of them succeeded in reaching the stricken ship and most of the men were saved.

Meanwhile the British *Calliope*, the highest powered of all the seven vessels, found that with full steam on the anchors were holding her from being driven back. With newly awakened hope her stokers redoubled their seemingly superhuman efforts. Slowly but surely she was gaining, her anchor chains slackened, the great "mud hooks" were hoisted, and though at first the gain was almost imperceptible it was real, and she was moving out to sea and comparative safety. With men and machines working at highest tension, she crept past the American ships, and the plucky lads trained under the Stars and Stripes, though they had reason to believe that they were facing death, stopped long enough to cheer sailors of another nation who were escaping the fate which awaited them, and as their applause arose above the tumult of roaring wind and water, the band played "Brittania rules the waves." Needless to say, the British sailors responded right lustily and their band played "Yankee Doodle." What voice could have failed to give the doomed men an encouraging cheer?

Instead of abating, the storm increased in intensity. Imagine a hurricane so fierce that powerful warships, with full steam on and three anchors down, cannot face it! It seems incredible. These vessels were as nearly invincible as human skill could make them, were manned by officers and crews trained for just such emergencies, but when actually pitted against omnipotent power they were as impotent as the frailest toy.

The watchers on shore saw the *Vandalia,* despite anchors and steam, drifting helplessly toward the coral reef which she finally struck stern first. Elder Dean's record says that each monster wave would pick her up and drop her onto the rocks until she was crushed, and settled down with decks just below the water. Hundreds of men were clinging to the rigging, many were swept overboard and some jumped hoping they could swim ashore, but the current carried most of them out to sea. The missionaries say that thirty or forty perished in this way before their eyes. They and the crowd lining the beach were as helpless as the ships themselves.

It is said that for more than thirty hours Rear Admiral Kimberly did not leave the bridge of his flagship *Trenton.* The storm played with her as a cat plays with a mouse. Time and again she made headway against the mountains of water which swept the decks; but each time when hope of reaching the open sea was highest the hurricane with tantalizing fury drove her back. As the darkness of Saturday night came on, the watchers could see her drifting helplessly down on the *Vandalia*, and the dawn of Sabbath morning revealed that the *Trenton*, notwithstanding her gallant fight, was also a wreck. Fortunately, however, by this time the storm had abated somewhat and all the men were saved. Previous to this the captain of the *Olga* following the example of the *Nipsic*, had voluntarily run ship onto the reef. None of his crew was lost.

Though six of the seven vessels went to pieces, the special missionaries were told by the captain of the *Tofua* that officers and men emerged the disaster with stainless names. During the weeks which elapsed before the United States could send other vessels to take away the stranded marines, they were royally entertained, and many tender, and a few pathetic, farewells were whispered when parting time finally came. The tragic story is current of a native girl who had fallen hopelessly in love with one of the officers and who wrote Samoa's favorite farewell song, "Tofa mai Feleni" (Good-bye, my friend). The tradition is that she swam after his vessel singing it as he sailed away, perhaps to another love, and to lands which to her were unknown. It is a beautiful song which quickly takes hold of one's heart, and if not equal to Hawaii's famous "Aloha Oe," it is a very close second.

Elder Dean concludes his interesting reference to the hurricane and the resultant loss of life with the laconic but significant sentence, "We brought home a cartload of wreckage."

The chief officer of the *Tofua* said that gales such as this are hurricanes in the South Seas, typhoons in the China Sea, monsoons in the Indian Ocean, cyclones in the Gulf of Mexico, and hell in all waters. He added with apparent earnestness that he had no intention of being profane, but such a storm at sea, as Sherman's definition of war, can be adequately described by that one word only.

One evening with this story still ringing in their ears, the special missionaries in company with President and Sister Adams, Brother and Sister Griffiths, President Coombs, and Elders Leland H. Stott and J. Kenneth Rallison passed these rusting hulks of warships and went aboard the diminutive gasoline launch, the *Marstal*, which had been engaged to carry them over to Pago Pago on the island of Tutuila. The weather was threatening and as the *Marstal* was absolutely without accommodations for passengers the sixteen hour ride was not viewed in the light of a pleasure excursion. But to preach the Gospel was Brother McKay's mission, all else was subordinate to that divine obligation.

The little boat possessed one redeeming feature—though she was tossed about on the waves like a cork, literally stirring the passengers to their very depths—one step brought the afflicted voyager to the vessel's side. As practically all of them had to reach the side pretty often and quickly, this was a distinct advantage. Oh, what a pitiably seasick lot they were! This malady came on insidiously, as temptation comes, and the party were like the man who could resist anything but temptation. Brother McKay usually does nothing by halves, but this occasion may have been an exception. Naturally no measurements were taken, but as nearly as one might estimate he divided himself about equally and threw away the "worser part."

Sister Thurza T. Adams showed her heroic and unselfish disposition. Though the sickest of the party, her thoughts during the entire night were for the comfort of everybody but herself. When the recording angel makes up his list of world heroines, the women who have labored as missionaries in the South Seas will surely be placed in an enviable position.

Before leaving port, Brother McKay had done a generous thing, and richly were he and his companions repaid for this act. The *Marstal* had been chartered to convey the missionaries to Pago Pago, wait until their work was completed and then bring them back to Apia, but just as they were ready to set sail the owner requested that the boat be permitted to return immediately with some freight and passengers. He promised to have it back in Pago Pago sufficiently early to meet Brother McKay's requirements. This consent was given. Among the passengers for whom this trip was made was Father Dennis O'Reilley, one of the Catholic priests to whom reference has heretofore been made. Subsequently he gave the following account of their experiences:

"We had hardly emerged from the harbor before we were soaked to the skin by rain and a few moments later by the waves which dashed completely over the tiny craft. During the night the engine balked and no amount of coaxing would induce it to go. There is only one thing worse in the world than sailing on the *Marstal* and that is being aboard her when she is not sailing, but is tossing wildly, but idly, in the rough open sea. Sunday morning found us still with a disabled engine, and completely out of sight of land. The captain, who travels about these islands with no other instrument than a compass, confessed complete ignorance as to our location. Though a sail was hoisted he had no idea as to the direction in which to steer. As evening approached, the boat was found to be leaking, and the captain abandoning hope said we should prepare for the worst.

"The natives aboard began saying good-bye to one another. However, being urged by the white passengers, the captain continued working on the engine, while crew and passengers took turns pumping. Before daylight of Monday morning the captain had the engine shooting, but very irregularly. After several hours we sighted land, and in the afternoon the *Marstal* limped through the coral reef and into the quiet little bay on the opposite side of the island from Apia, to which point my companion and I walked the following day."

An experience similar to this would doubtless have come to the brethren had the boat waited until they were ready to return. Instead she came, though two days late, with a repaired and properly working engine.

However, before this happened the missionary party chugged along the green coast of Tutuila en route to Pago Pago. The suggestion that it is wondrously beautiful made by one of the voyagers, who, however, was not sufficiently enthusiastic to raise his head to behold the grandeur he described, had little effect, for the rest of the party neither knew nor cared whether or not it was beautiful.

A haggard, weary, and disconsolate looking lot landed under the Stars and Stripes which somewhat revived their drooping spirits, and these were almost completely restored by the hearty welcome given there at the conference house by President William S. Muir and his hospitable wife, Edna Walton Muir.

The Church owns a long time lease on a large plantation, consisting principally of coconut trees, at Maupusaga about twelve miles from Pago Pago, and here one of the best Church schools on the islands is maintained. The school band, under the leadership of Elder Lorenzo E. Peterson, and a multitude of members and friends headed by Elder William C. Brewer and Harry S. Jacobs extended a welcome as hearty, if not so elaborate, as any extended the special missionaries. Many distant as well as nearby villages were represented by their chiefs and chosen "Taupos" (Virgins).

The days spent here were full of delightful experiences. Meetings were held, instructions given, and testimonies borne. The joy manifested by these humble people at the privilege of shaking hands with one of the general authorities cannot be described. The more phlegmatic whites of the Church, both in Zion and abroad, might with profit have viewed this demonstration.

The need of more and better schools was apparent. Scarcely one of the Elders was a trained teacher, and still it was really surprising how well they were doing. The following translated petition will perhaps be of interest:

"Tutuila, Samoa, May 23, 1921.

"To His Excellency, the Prophet,

"Church of Jesus Christ of Latter-day Saints

"This will be presented to Apostle McKay and President Adams of the Samoan Mission.

"Your Highness;

"We petition you with respect and deference and due honor as follows:

"We respectfully and in love request you to kindly accede to our desires that you send us some school teachers for the school in Maupusaga. We know assuredly that this is the one way in which the inhabitants of this island can quickly obtain knowledge, and by this acquisition of knowledge men will be made acquainted with the Gospel.

"If it is in accordance with your will, please send some male teachers for the boys, and lady teachers for the girls.

"We have prepared this petition with sincerity in our hearts; we depend upon your great love to receive our request.

"Soifua, (May you be blessed).

"We are the High Chiefs and authorities of the church in Tutuila."

This was presented by twenty-five chiefs.

At the conclusion of the conference and their inspection of the school and the plantation, the special missionaries left Maupusaga ahead of the main body of visitors. After their departure one of the native boys, who was to assist in carrying the satchels, said: "We must hurry, for the 'Apostolo' and Brother Cannon have gone. It has stopped raining now, but it will start again as soon as they reach Pago Pago. If we are not there by that time we will get wet." And Sister Adams added, "Do you hear that? I believe it, and I'm not going to wait for breakfast."

The boy's statement proved to be correct. No sooner were the missionaries in the conference house than the rain descended in floods.

Some readers of this narrative may not know that the United States controls American Samoa, using it as a naval base. It consists of the islands of Tutuila, Manua, Olosega, Ofu, Annuu and the uninhabited coral atoll Rose Island, with a total population of about 7,500. At the time of this visit Captain Waldo Evans was governor, and a pleasant interview was had with him and with the Superintendent of Instruction and also the Minister of Native Affairs. The relation of Church schools to the government, uniform textbooks, and other important matters were profitably discussed.

It was 9 p.m. when the *Marstal* with the tired party of missionaries reached Apia on the return voyage, and it was feared that they would have to spend another night on the uncomfortable boat, but thanks to the intervention of United States Consul Roberts and the consequent courtesy of the custom officials the offices were kept open for their benefit and they were thus permitted to land. Another courteous thing was done. The captain of the mail boat *Ajax* delayed his departure from Apia for more than two hours, thinking perhaps the brethren might have some mail which they desired to send out.

Crowd at Mission Home, Apia, Samoa

CHAPTER 16

SAUNIATU

"This is moral perfection: to live each day as though it were the last; to be tranquil, yet not indifferent to our fate."

—Marcus Aurelius

Among white races one often hears the statement that the Gospel deprives men of liberty and makes slaves of them. The Samoans, even non-members of the Church, view this differently and, in truth, more sensibly. They consider that man a slave who uses tobacco or liquor and cannot overcome the habit, accepting literally the Savior's words: "Whosoever committeth sin is the servant of sin. . . . If the Son therefore shall make you free, ye shall be free indeed" (John 8:34, 36).

Because of the childlike and inspiring faith of the Islanders the Lord gives them unusual manifestations as He did the Lamanites, their ancestors, whenever they humbled themselves and came to him in faith. Almost every Church member can tell of something supernatural through which he was made to understand the plan of salvation, and these stories are related with a sincerity which banishes doubt as to their genuineness.

Sauniatu is the principal branch of the Church in Samoa. Here the best school on the islands is located, and the Church owns a large plantation of coconut trees. Brothers McKay and Cannon and

President and Sister Adams rode on horseback to this place. The trail over which they traveled skirted the seacoast, sometimes along sandy beaches, and occasionally over precipitous cliffs. The intense blueness of the sky, the still deeper blue of the water, the thundering surf on the coral reef, magnificent trees of every tropical variety, among which the stately coconut palms predominated, will never be forgotten by those who have the good fortune to pass that way. Everywhere natives were gathering and breaking coconuts for the market. It would surprise a European to see how completely these nuts cover the ground. There were literally millions and millions of them, and preparing them for shipment is one of the chief occupations of the people. Reference has heretofore been made to the thirst-quenching liquid which these nuts contain. The natives are very proficient in selecting those of proper ripeness and are always ready to climb a tree to obtain for a stranger the very best drink which can be had. On a hot day, and there are no days in Samoa which are not hot, this beverage is very refreshing.

Word had evidently gone ahead that "Apostolo" McKay was coming, for in every village groups of curious and in most cases reverential people were gathered. Many of these were not affiliated with the Church, but our members are held in high esteem, and it was easy for the natives to revere one of their leaders. In the village of Fusi, in which place no Mormons were living, the men all stood at attention as the missionary party drew near. At a word of command, they saluted, many of them kneeling as they did so. It was a mark of courtesy which was the more appreciated because it was so spontaneous and unexpected.

The distance between Apia and Sauniatu is twenty long miles, and the luggage of the missionaries was carried on the shoulders of young natives who walked the entire distance barefooted and kept pace with those on horseback. The regrets which Brother McKay felt at seeing these sturdy fellows walking while he rode were dissipated during succeeding days, for those who had performed this arduous task were considered by all as having been especially favored. Among those who walked also were a number of elders, and as the visiting brethren looked at the hardy young chaps they saw ample justification for the pride the Church feels in its missionaries. As a rule they are as pure-minded and clean in thought and act as maidens; sturdy, virile, and physically fit as any men in the world; men who dare to do right and with a courage which enables them to face any difficulty, including the scorn of the thoughtless or ignorant; men who would go to the ends of the earth if they were asked; so self-sacrificing that they will walk miles to preach the Gospel of Christ to an investigator or to administer to an unknown afflicted person; young men appreciative of the fact that their parents, or not infrequently widowed mothers, are working longer hours than they should, wearing shabby clothes, staying awake nights planning how to make ends meet and keep their sons in the field; men who would not only die for their faith, but who live for it. These are they whom the world stamps as wicked impostors who are laying snares to entangle the feet of their fellow men. How incredibly blind!

From the village of Fusi, one of the high chiefs accompanied the party to its destination, and at his order some of his people brought presents of mats, many kinds of fruits, and other food, among which was a whole roasted pig.

At the Sauniatu plantation, the party was met by a group of missionaries and Church members headed by Elder Ray W. Berrett, president of the conference. Brother McKay's description of the welcome follows:

"As we walked slowly toward the conference house, the band struck up 'The Star Spangled Banner.' To hear that old air away off here in Samoa, played so impressively by Samoan boys, to see the women of the village, all dressed in white and men well dressed standing in line opposite the women; to walk along a well-cleaned roadway strewn on each side with palm branches; to realize that every heart was beating a welcome, even though it was accompanied by a feeling of curiosity, made me feel that this simple unostentatious greeting from the little village of Sauniatu was one of the most impressive of our entire trip. My feelings were stirred and found expression in a tear or two that trickled over the eyelids."

The three days which followed were among the most memorable of this memorable journey. With feasts and concerts, with native dances and gifts of fruit, beads, and mats, the good people endeavored to show their appreciation of the visit. And these tokens of goodwill did not come solely from Church members. Many delegations headed by their chiefs and made up entirely of non-members came with songs, speeches, dances, and gifts.

The spirit of the Lord was remarkably manifest in the meetings, and instructions were given which those in attendance will never forget. The Sunday School deserves special mention. While the organist played, the people of the village led by a little girl came marching in, graded in size from the baby up to the adult.

The people carried neatly folded mats under their arms and these when spread on the cement floor furnished seats for the congregation. This organization is impressing upon the hearts of old and young lessons of priceless value. In these gatherings taro, the root of a plant, is used instead of bread for the sacrament.

Brother McKay and five other missionaries were guests at the home of Brother Sai Masina and family. This was the first individual Samoan family to entertain in real native fashion one of the general authorities. The travelers had been in many Samoan huts and had participated in greater feasts, but this was purely a family affair and was typically characteristic of the South Seas.

As the party approached the hut with its open sides and its thatched roof, resembling that of a miniature tabernacle set on upright posts, the family arose and the children sang a song of welcome.

Mats were spread upon the clean pebble floor and these were bounteously covered with taro, chicken, plates of soup, pork, cocoa, pudding, coconuts, bananas, and other fruits. Of course it was necessary to sit cross-legged on the ground while partaking of this repast.

Though inclined to postpone the hour of departure from this interesting village, the time for parting came at last. Speeches were made by the orators and chiefs of this and surrounding villages.

Chief Fa'ifai, a non-member of the Church, closed his remarks with tears in his eyes and with these words:

"Our hearts are broken to hear your parting words. . . . We request that when you return to Zion and meet the Prophet and the Quorum of the Twelve that you put Samoa in your hearts as a seal. May your Excellencies be blessed, also President Adams and Mrs. Adams as well as all the elders and saints."

The actual departure of the brethren was delayed for more than an hour while they administered to afflicted children and adults. This duty finally accomplished, Brother McKay and his party emerged from the back room of the conference house and were at once overwhelmed by crowds awaiting them in the front room. The Relief Society sisters and others began a farewell song, accompanied by the band, but weeping soon took the place of singing. Many knelt and kissed the hands of the visitors and bathed them in tears.

A former statement may properly be repeated, that these people had looked forward with as much anticipation to Brother McKay's visit as a white race would display while awaiting one of the ancient Apostles if they knew through prophecy that he would appear in his resurrected form at a given date. To illustrate this statement: Chief Sai Masina, eighty-four years old, at whose home the brethren had been entertained, as he knelt and kissed Brother McKay's hand said with tears streaming down his furrowed cheeks, "My prayers have been answered; I have seen an Apostle of the Lord, and now I am ready to go." The first word the brethren received after they had finally left the islands was that this good man had passed on to his reward.

Their own feelings deeply stirred and with bedimmed eyes the visitors pressed through the crowds and mounted the horses which were in waiting. The people followed them across the bridge which spans the beautiful stream and the band played "Tofa mai Feleni" (Good-bye, my friend). As Brother McKay looked back through the avenue of trees and saw the band and crowd following, he felt impressed to return and offer a prayer with them, and this inspiration was immediately followed.

As he prayed for and blessed the multitude, one was unconsciously reminded of that touching farewell which the Savior took of the people, as recorded in the Book of Mormon, Third Nephi, chapters 17 and 18. Though the Christ was not present in person, he was represented by a divinely chosen servant and his comforting spirit was felt by all. Later it was learned that the prayer had been written, as nearly as it could be remembered by Brother Sua Kippen and others, and was placed in the cornerstone of an impressive monument which was erected on the place.

Here was seen a splendid example of the fact that the Gospel of Jesus Christ makes one of all mankind. These people were strangers to the visitors. They had never met until a few days previously; they were of a different race, with different language, color, and customs. One thing only was held in common—their faith—and yet genuine tears of sorrow were shed on each side at parting. It was an affecting and unforgettable experience.

In Apia the day before departure of Brother McKay's party from Samoa, eighteen missionaries and a host of natives sat down in the commodious home of Brother Ah Ching, a full-blooded Chinese and a faithful member of the Church. He is a wealthy man and his auto was always at the disposal of the brethren. One of his sons has been educated in China with the thought that he may be needed later as a missionary to that land. The story of this man's life reads like a novel. He was cook for a long time on a ship, and with typical Chinese thrift had saved three thousand dollars. This was entrusted to a confidential friend, but the money was dishonestly used and lost to Brother Ching. At the time, he was not a member of the Church and made up his mind to kill the man who had thus wronged him, and for this purpose he obtained a long knife "as sharp as a razor." Then something came over him which caused a complete change of heart. He decided to permit the man to live, though he felt sure the untrue friend would always be rich while he himself would always remain poor. However, the anticipated conditions were exactly reversed. He had become rich while the man who robbed him had come many times as a beggar to his door, and, be it said to the credit of this faithful Chinese brother, that his former enemy was always given clothing and food.

There were present at this feast, in addition to names mentioned elsewhere in this chronicle, Elders Ralph A. Knowlton, Arthur Huntsman, Lewis B. Parkin, and Ralph Putnam.

During this same entertainment another Church member who had been an officer on a small trading schooner told of a visit to the Phoenix group of islands, where he had witnessed a dangerous method of fishing for sharks. These fish were very numerous in the harbor, but were shy and would not come near enough to the fishing boat to be speared. At last the natives tied a rope about the waist of one of their number who jumped into the water. The sharks darted for him, and as he was jerked violently into the boat a dozen hungry jaws snapped at the spot where a moment before his legs had been. By means of this human bait the natives were able to throw their spears into the backs of these fish.

Despite their frequency, the touching farewells which the visitors experienced in the South Seas never become commonplace. It was no easier to say good-bye to the friends in Apia than it had been in other places. These faithful souls acknowledged in Brother McKay's visit an answer to prayer; they had listened to inspired words and had received additional confirmation of their faith that the Almighty does have divinely chosen men to lead his people.

Boys comprising the school band had walked the twenty miles from Sauniatu carrying their instruments, even the big bass drum, in order to cheer the travelers on their way.

It was dark when the brethren boarded the *Tofua*. Their cabin was filled with fruits and flowers. Many members and friends accompanied them on board and could hardly be induced to leave when the last bugle sounded warning that the vessel was about to sail. The band and crowds of members and friends were on the pier and strains of music from instruments and voices accompanied the ship as it sailed out into the night.

Elder David O. McKay & President Hugh
J. Cannon on Horseback, Sauniatu

Band, Sauniatu

Men Working on Monument, Sauniatu

Time for Departure, Sauniautu, Samoa

CHAPTER 17

TONGA

"Your sole contribution to the sum of things is yourself."
— Frank Crane

Brother McKay entertained the hope that the quarantine which prevented his party while en route to Samoa from landing in Tonga would be raised and that they could land on the return journey, a hope encouraged by officers of the vessel. It proved, however, to be fallacious. The *Tofua* stopped at Vavau, which had lost none of its romantic beauty since the previous visit, and meetings might have been held. But no one was permitted to land. This experience was repeated at Haapai, another island of the Tongan group where there is a branch of the Church. It became evident that the only way to visit these islands was to go into quarantine for two weeks at Nukualofa. This meant that passengers would be held literally as prisoners on a little island in the harbor. A native would be sent out from the mainland to cook, and here the passengers could "sit and think," or when tired of that, could just "sit."

It was interesting to watch the struggle through which Brother McKay passed. The work awaiting the brethren in New Zealand furnished ample excuse for his going on and leaving Brother Cannon to visit these islands. To his restless spirit the thought of remaining almost in complete idleness for two weeks was well nigh maddening. The reality of it, he feared, would be quite so. Naturally the desirable and comfortable thing to do was to proceed with the *Tofua*. But he knew these people, as those of the other islands, had been expecting to see one of the Twelve and would be bitterly disappointed with a substitute. Resisting his own personal inclinations, therefore, he decided to remain and have Brother Cannon go on to New Zealand to which point he would follow as soon as possible.

President Mark V. Coombs, having been in Samoa, was also obliged to go into quarantine as were the newly arrived missionaries, Clarence Henderson, Walter J. Phillips, Lewis B. Parkin, and George T. Robinson. Upon the arrival of the vessel at Nukualofa, they and about thirty other unfortunates were loaded into a barge which was towed across the bay to the quarantine island.

Ordinarily such isolation would have furnished excellent opportunities for preaching the Gospel to fellow prisoners, and, even with a rather serious handicap, before they were finally released a number of lasting friendships had been made. Most readers of this narrative already know that Brother McKay is a "good mixer." In this instance his task was a difficult one, for two of the passengers with him and his party were Wesleyan ministers who were horrified when they learned that a fellow prisoner professed to be an Apostle of the Lord Jesus Christ; and so strong was their prejudice that it was not easy for them to be decently civil. Naturally they had considerable influence over a number of those present. Nevertheless the uniform courtesy of the missionaries, the spirit with which they sang the hymns of Zion, always a potent means of overcoming opposition, and the consistency of the doctrines were irresistible. At some of the services which were held many "who came to scoff, remained to pray."

Naturally such ministers were not happy in Brother McKay's presence. When the counterfeit is placed side by side with the genuine the contrast is too marked, and the feelings of these men were probably similar to those they will have hereafter should they be permitted to come into the presence of apostles and prophets.

More deep-seated opposition to the restored Gospel is met in Tonga than in other island groups of the South Seas. Representatives of various denominations have done considerable work among the natives with the result that there is much disunion among them, but they fraternize in a manner worthy of a better cause whenever it is possible to do or say anything against the Mormons. If further evidence were needed of the divinity of this work, it could be found in the sudden unity which occurs among man-made systems whenever they come in contact with truths revealed anew in this dispensation. In Tonga all the leading men of the islands were invited to attend the meetings, but, unlike the Samoans, none of them responded.

Brother McKay was able, however, to have a profitable interview with the Prince Consort, Uiliamo Tugi, upon whom he made an excellent impression, according to the report of President Coombs, who was present during the conversation. The Prince said the sole objection to the preaching of Mormonism on the islands was that it took too many members from the Protestant churches.

The reception given to the visitor on these islands resembled those accorded him in Samoa. All wanted to press his hand and no one was denied the privilege. An old lady who had been sickly for some time reported that she felt entirely well after having grasped his hand.

The story is told of another lady, a non-member, who had been investigating the Gospel and who desired to have Brother McKay administer to her. The Elders knew her as an inveterate smoker, and one of them suggested that she should observe the Word of Wisdom before making such a request.

"But I do keep the Word of Wisdom," was her response. "Indeed? When did you quit smoking?" asked the missionary.

"Last night," came the unabashed reply.

After holding conference in Nukualofa, it was decided to visit branches in Haapai and Vavau on the other islands, and a small two mast schooner was chartered. There were in the party, besides Brother McKay, President Coombs and his wife and three small children, three missionaries, and several natives. The following is taken from President Coombs' account of the trip:

"All the Saints were at the wharf to see us off, while some of the more venturesome boys came aboard the vessel and remained until we were nearly a mile out to sea, when with a farewell wave of the hand they dove from the top of the mast and swam ashore.

"We were no sooner outside the protecting reefs than a strong wind sprang up. How the boat did rock! We were nearly all sick. The writer was so sick that he could not help his wife. She was so sick that she would not look after the children. But the natives came to the rescue and tended the babies as though they were their own.

"More than once during the night huge waves swept completely over us, wetting us through and through. Elders Clark and Oborn were nearly washed overboard, and would have been lost, but fortunately they became entangled in the rigging which held them on. A mountainous wave washed the only lifeboat loose, and it crushed a poor old woman's foot so badly that she was in the hospital for eight weeks.

"During all this time the captain had tied the helm and was letting the boat drift with no hand to guide it. He had commenced to drink and thought more of his liquor than he did of the lives of his passengers. Seeing that something must be done, Brother McKay finally took the bottle from him by force, and though deathly seasick himself was compelled to watch the captain during the whole of that stormy night to prevent him from becoming too drunk to navigate the vessel.

"So we sailed all that night and the next day. It was not until eight o'clock in the evening that we landed at Haapai. We held meeting with the Saints there and prepared to leave the next morning at daybreak for Vavau. When morning came, however, it was discovered that the heavy seas of the night before had split the rudder so that it had to be repaired.

"It was two o'clock in the afternoon before we finally set out. Again as soon as we were outside the reef an extremely heavy wind arose. We expected to make Vavau that night, but the captain, again under the influence of liquor, set the course too far to the west, so that when evening came no Vavau was in sight, and we did not know where we were. We tacked back and forth all night, and when morning came instead of seeing Vavau we could see the island of Leyte and realized that we were fifty miles off our course. However, it was a consolation to know our whereabouts, and we were a very thankful party of people when we came alongside the Vavau wharf at three o'clock in the afternoon, nearly twenty-four hours after the expected time of arrival."

Traveling to and from these islands one hears even yet many heartrending stories of suffering and death which occurred during the years 1918 and 1919 when the "flu" spread over the earth with such devastating results. The mortality among Church members was notably less than among those not of our faith, and many remarkable cases of healing are related. Nevertheless there were numerous fatalities even among the Latter-day Saints, and one missionary, Elder Langston, succumbed to the malady. It seems necessary in fulfillment of the Lord's plan that some of his servants lay down their lives as evidence of their sincerity of purpose in every land where the Gospel is being preached. Though Elder Langston's voice is stilled, his testimony will ever live. His parents have sent a fitting headstone for his grave, and he sleeps in that beautiful and restful place, among the people whose salvation was dearer to him and to his associates than were their own lives. This faithful missionary was properly buried, for his co-laborers performed that task, though they themselves were weak from disease.

A law in Tonga provides that every young man upon attaining his majority shall be given a piece of land of sufficient size, if it be properly cultivated, to maintain a family. This he cannot legally sell, though under some circumstances it may be leased. Thus every Tongan becomes a freeholder. The story was told Brother McKay of a young native of high birth who had joined the Church. He was offered large tracts of land, in addition to that which would naturally come to him, and a very desirable position in the government as well, if he would but relinquish his Church membership; but he unhesitatingly replied that he would not exchange the joy which the Gospel gave for the entire Tongan group and all their wealth. He was alike unmoved by the pleadings of former friends and offer of

Elder McKay and Tongan Women

position and riches. He, as all who actually receive the testimony of the spirit, knew he had received something more priceless than wealth or the transitory honor of men.

While Brother McKay was passing through these stirring experiences in Tonga, Brother Cannon was having an uneventful voyage toward New Zealand. To one who has been promised that if he is seasick "it will be of very short duration," ocean travel is delightful. It would have been particularly so on this trip except that the brethren had been together so much it seemed unnatural to be traveling alone.

Only two things occurred which were out of the ordinary. When Brother McKay left the ship at Nukualofa, two young men were put in the cabin with Brother Cannon. One of these seemed from the first to be far from normal, and the other who was acquainted with him did not conceal his fear that something might happen. It did. The young man had been acting strangely all day, and during the night he completely lost his mind and began to rave. The captain was called and the poor fellow was locked up in a padded cell and remained there until Auckland was reached.

While nearing Suva, the *Tofua* received word that the *Attua*, a sister ship belonging to the Burns-Philps line, had run onto the beach at Naitonitoni, about a hundred miles distant. Her captain, endeavoring to save a few miles of travel, had cut so close to the reef that he struck it a glancing blow which tore a great hole in the side of his vessel. By closing the watertight doors and confining the water to one compartment the ship was able to sail four miles and there they had been compelled to beach her. No lives were lost but many hundreds of tons of sugar were destroyed.

The *Tofua* made a hurried run to Naitonitoni and picked up the passengers as well as a large amount of uninjured sugar. In addition to this cargo, at Suva the *Tofua* took on eighteen thousand cases of bananas and an enormous number of bunches which were not cased, as well as several thousand cases of oranges.

President L.H. Kennard, of the Tahitian Mission, had come to New Zealand in accordance with instructions from Brother McKay, and he and Brother Cannon spent some little time in securing figures from shipbuilding firms for a schooner for use in the Tahitian islands.

In company with President George S. Taylor and his estimable wife, Brother Cannon attended conferences in Thames, where the branch is made up of whites, and Omahu, where the membership is almost wholly native. In the former place President Benjamin Brown and Elders James A. Thornton, Francis L. Wilcox, and Ray Nelson were laboring and in the latter the visitors met President Alvin T. Maughan and Elder William J. Warner.

It is not always pleasant to sleep with comparative strangers, but Brother Cannon felt greatly blessed in having the privilege of sleeping with President Brown. All day long he had been almost devoured by fleas. He managed to rid himself of a few of these tormenting pests while preparing for bed but no sooner were the covers pulled up over him than he felt them in large and industrious numbers. Brother Brown soon came to bed, and these pests instantly left Brother Cannon, much to his relief. They had found someone more to their liking. The next morning when Brother Brown showed the marks of battle on his legs and body, Brother Cannon felt somewhat conscience-smitten, but still declares he will never miss an opportunity of sleeping with Brother Brown if they are in a country where fleas abound.

Any native New Zealander will scoff at the suggestion that America's Yellowstone is comparable for a moment with their famed Rotorua. The two places are not unlike. In each, one has the same feeling that the earth may suddenly open up or explode or perform some other unnatural and dangerous feat, but the true American is just as certain that there is no comparison between the two places as is the New Zealander. The visit to Rotorua was made on the first of July, almost midwinter in this hemisphere, and it was extremely cold, especially for one who had just come from the tropics.

CHAPTER 18

AUCKLAND, NEW ZEALAND

"The only sacrifice which Jesus asked of his people was the same sacrifice which the farmer makes when he throws his seed into the soil."

—Roger Babson

Much might be written about the famous thermal region of Rotorua, its geysers and hot pots, its villages where all the cooking, as well as the family washing, is done in the boiling springs, and where the natives warm themselves by sitting on hot rocks. The visitor hears of the wonderful pink and white terraces, destroyed more than two score years ago by a terrible volcano and series of earthquakes.

Space will not permit of even a passing reference to many of these things and fortunately it is unnecessary as better descriptions than one could hope to give here may be found elsewhere.

While awaiting Brother McKay's return to New Zealand, Brother Cannon was guest at the Mission Home in Auckland and was made welcome by President and Sister Taylor and their two daughters as well as by Secretary Frederick W. Schwendiman and his wife, President Joseph Anderson, Wallace L. Castleton, Heber Dean Hall, and Abram M. McFarlane who were living there.

One evening he and some of these brethren were invited to have supper with Brother and Sister Kewene, a Maori family. Upon their arrival, they found the family greatly excited and learned that a few moments before, a fire had broken out in the home. A lighted candle had been left in an open window of the room where their baby was sleeping; the wind had blown the curtain into the flame and from this the blaze started. A neighbor across the way, seeing the trouble, sent his little boy over to tell the people their house was on fire. The little chap walked around the building to the back door and knocked timidly. His knock was answered by one of the boys of the family and the messenger asked to see the father, and when he finally came he was told the house was on fire. The little babe was almost suffocated when they rushed in, and it was revived with the utmost difficulty.

After Brother McKay's return from Tonga to New Zealand, conferences were held in Auckland and in the Ngapuhi, Porirua, Dannevirke, and Hastings Districts. Varied experiences were had in each of these places, many meetings were held, and the visitors were entertained in royal native style. Numberless noses were pressed, and the wild "Haka" and the graceful "Poi" dances were witnessed.

One of the meetings in Auckland was disturbed by a number of Reorganites who had come with their usual challenge to a public debate. Missionaries are accustomed to meeting a spirit of hatred, but it is seldom found in more virulent type than among these people. Satan knows full well that the more truth is mixed with his falsehoods the more dangerous it is, and he surely has prepared a poisonous mixture for those who listen to those people. Brother McKay handled the situation with a dignity which won the following remark from a gentleman as he shook hands cordially: "Good-bye, I wish you success. I like your style."

While in Auckland the special missionaries saw Elders Roland C. Parry and Warren J. Stallings, who had just been released, depart on their journey around the world. They also said good-bye to Elder Milton Hall who, almost protestingly, was leaving for home because of ill health.

They were also entertained by Mr. Walter E. Bush, city engineer of Auckland, who had been in Salt Lake and while there had formed the acquaintance of Bishop Sylvester Q. Cannon who at that time was city engineer. The visitors listened to an address which he made before the Rotary Club of Auckland in which he showed some of New Zealand's latent possibilities, particularly in the line of undeveloped power projects. It was surprising to learn that Auckland has almost trebled in size in the fourteen years prior to this visit.

At Ngapuhi the travelers met Brother Joseph Hay. This man has a unique profession. He obtains a lease on a forest of the stately and useful kauri trees and at a certain season climbs the trees and cuts into the bark in various places. A few months later he again climbs them and gathers the gum which has exuded from the wounds. The man has a rope looped around the tree and encircling his waist. He has sharp hooks made for his hands and wears a clog on each foot with a spike in it and these enable him to walk up the side of a kauri tree, whose nearest branches are sometimes sixty feet from the ground, with as much apparent ease as an ordinary person ascends a flight of stairs. New Zealanders are justifiably proud of the kauri. According to reports it is not uncommon for one of them to contain 15,000 feet of lumber.

The thoughtful kindness manifested by the natives to strangers is often very touching. For instance at one of the entertainments, the visitors were sitting in the open air, listening to speeches which were being made in their honor, when a grey-haired, sweet-faced old lady, the mother of Brother Stewart Meha who had distinguished himself in translating for the brethren, came with a pot of burning charcoal and placed it at their feet. As the weather was really chilly the warmth from these coals was appreciated, but the loving solicitude of this gentle native sister will be remembered long after the physical warmth has been forgotten.

Apparently nothing gives the Maoris greater pleasure than to prepare a big banquet. The excellent quality of the food served is only surpassed by the quantity, and the visitor scarcely leaves the table at one meal before preparations are begun for the next. This was particularly true at the homes of Brothers Elliot Nopera and William Duncan, both full-blooded Maoris and an honor to their race. Both have beautiful homes. At both places Brother McKay and party were taken from the station in large, high powered automobiles belonging to these brethren. The visitors were each given a room furnished so well as to cause Brother McKay to remark, "If these people should ever visit me I could not give them as good a room as this."

Brother Nopera's place is on the outskirts of Dannevirke. When asked how many acres he had in the farm, the good brother appeared to be a little puzzled, but at last he understood.

"Oh, this isn't my farm, this is my city place. I have only three hundred acres here."

"How many acres have you in your farm?" Brother McKay asked in surprise.

"I have nine hundred acres in the farm proper, but there are several thousands acres of grazing lands connected with it."

The home of Brother William Duncan is also a commodious one and it, and everything else he has in the world, is at the disposal of the Church. From his house to the railway station the visitors had a thrilling ride. To *Hangi* and say good-bye to those assembled had required so much time that the roar of the express train, with which they were scheduled to travel, was heard in the distance as they entered the waiting auto. The handsome young Maori, William Duncan, at the wheel promised to beat the train to the station which was about two miles distant. And how he did drive! And what a picture he made with his curling hair, dark skin, flashing eyes, and beautiful teeth whenever he glanced back to see how near the train was! At last Brother McKay wisely suggested that he would watch the train if the driver would watch the road.

The principal Church school in New Zealand is at Hastings and is rated as an Agricultural College. Good work was being done by this institution which had been under the direction of Principal Franklin E. Stott, though at the time of this visit Elder Leo B. Sharp arrived to take over this position as Brother Stott was about to be released. Brother Sharp had declined an offer of a position with the Ames Agricultural College in order to fill this mission. His wife accompanied him and during the very first day of her mission displayed qualities, as the other lady missionaries had already done, which stamped her as a real missionary. With Brother Sharp were Elders Merrill, Hollingworth, and Jorgenson, the last named brother being appointed to take the place of Elder Fisher as teacher in the school. Other brethren who were engaged either in the school or on the mission paper were Elders Erwin W. Meser, Jos. M. Stephenson, F. Anderwon, Glenn B. Cannon, Paul R. Buttle, Henry J. Armstrong, Richard G. Andrew, and Amasa S. Holmes.

A great celebration was held at the College in honor of the visitors. Oratory is a highly prized gift among the natives and apparently they begin early to develop it. The speeches and other program numbers furnished by native students were very creditable. At the conclusion of the regular exercises and at a signal from their class leader—a young Maori, not a Church member but who only awaited his father's consent to be baptized—a group of stalwart boys seized Brother McKay and hoisting him high in the air while another group carried Brother Cannon in the same perilous position they galloped around the hall singing, "For he's a jolly good fellow." Though appreciative of this high honor, the honored ones considered it too high and felt more comfortable when occupying a more lowly position.

Though feasts among the Maoris play an important role in all social events, they do not always think of eating. Sunday is almost invariably a fast day with them. Going without food is preferable to preparing it on the Sabbath day, and even in the evening when their fast is broken, they eat simple things which have been prepared previously.

Indeed, all through New Zealand, the people show a very commendable respect for the Lord's day. Except on the trunk line between Wellington and Auckland, no trains run on that day. And, although commendable, it was very inconvenient for the visitors, for they had engaged passage on the *Ulimaroa* which was to leave Auckland Tuesday morning, and in order to make proper preparations for departure, it was necessary to take the night train.

But there was no night train from Hastings to Palmerstone North, a distance of 112 miles. Brother Duncan and others offered to hire an auto, as none of them had theirs along, but the price asked was exorbitant. However, Mr. Webb, a very courteous gentleman who was in the meeting at Dannevirke, had driven to Hastings again to attend the service and insisted on taking the brethren in his Hudson to Palmerstone North where they could board the midnight train for Auckland. Many Church members would balk at a drive of 224 miles to accommodate strangers. Mr. Webb not only did this, but waited at the station until the train came shortly before one o'clock a.m. in order to have a few moments longer with Brother McKay.

During this visit to New Zealand, and in addition to those whose names are mentioned elsewhere in this volume, the special missionaries met the following Elders: James A. Rawson, Edward M. Stanger, Peter M. Johnson, Leon Willie, Melvin C. Stewart, William H. Clark, Russell Lane, Warren Tonks, Jonathan R. Bennett, Gerald F. Heaton, Ralph R. Baird, Ephraim R. Nelson, Harold Hawkes, Joseph E. Francom, Donald L. Hunsaker, Joseph R. Egbert, Ernest A. Ottley, Newel S. Brown, Hyrum V. Bell, Edgar W. Barber, Jacob I. Smith, George S. Winn, Leo E. Coombs, Earl A. Frederickson, Lonell W. Miller, Harold Jenkins, Heber Hymas, Frank L. Crockett, Carlos W. Clark, William Arley Cole, and Arthur W. Gudmanson.

The farewells in New Zealand were perhaps not so demonstrative as were those of some other isles, but were quite as affecting. Here, too, tears were shed, and the sorrow which these good people felt in parting was as sincere as that manifested in any land.

The journey to Sydney, Australia, ordinarily requires four days. In this instance five were consumed because of a terrific storm which prevailed. At several meals not more than a dozen people appeared, though there were more than three hundred passengers aboard. During one entire day not more than seven passengers were in the dining room at one time, and at one meal only three were present. President Lund's promise still held, and Brother Cannon was one of the three.

CHAPTER 19

AUSTRALIA

"Courage and perseverance have a magical talisman, before which difficulties disappear and obstacles vanish into air."

—John Quincy Adams

Sydney, Australia, formerly Port Jackson, boasts of having one of the finest landlocked harbors in the world. It has nearly two hundred miles of waterfront and is so deep that the largest steamers can draw up to piers within a very few moments' walking distance of the busiest business district.

As the storm-tossed Ulimaroa entered this peaceful haven on a smiling Sabbath day, the passengers felt they were emerging from a tempestuous world into a veritable Garden of Eden. This comparison might well have occurred to them because of the change in weather conditions, but a contributing cause was found as their eyes searched the rapidly approaching shore and on their right they saw wandering about in apparently untrammeled freedom all manner of wild animals: lions, tigers, bears, and other things which go to make up a well-equipped Eden—or a modern zoo. As the steamer drew nearer, and even with the aid of binoculars, passengers failed to discern anything resembling a cage. A subsequent visit to the place, however, revealed deep and impassable cement trenches which kept the animals within bounds.

At the landing stage, the brethren were met by President Don C. Rushton of the Australian Mission and several other missionaries.

The Church members in Australia are all white, practically no work having been done among the aborigines. The welcome extended the visitors at Mission headquarters by Sister Rushton and a number of assembled Saints was no whit less sincere, even though less demonstrative, than those witnessed among the Polynesians. For the first time in this dispensation, or in any other as far as we have record, one of the general authorities had set foot on this land. Naturally the Latter-day Saints rejoiced to meet Brother McKay, at first because of his exalted position, but afterwards because of his personality which instantly won their hearts.

It was the first Sunday in August, consequently fast day, and Brother McKay expressed the desire to hear the members bear testimony. It was a source of joy to find here in the Antipodes the same positive knowledge of the divinity of this work that is so noticeable in other climes. Many people belonging to other churches believe, most of them in a rather superficial way, that their religion is true; but how rarely is one found who claims through prayer and study to have gained an absolute and personal testimony from the Almighty on this point? That vital and compelling conviction is usually absent. On the other hand, how seldom is a Latter-day Saint of mature age found who does not know that the Father and the Son appeared to Joseph Smith, that through them and their subsequent messengers the Gospel, with all its saving graces, was restored to earth!

This special mission demonstrated that the knowledge of the Almighty and his divine plan has spread abroad, and Isaiah's words are gradually being fulfilled: "The earth shall be full of the knowledge of the Lord, as the waters cover the sea" (Isaiah 11:9).

Who has not heard of Port Jackson, Botany Bay, Van Dieman's land? As is generally well known, Australia was once England's convict settlement. To this country offenders were banished, and naturally the early history abounds in tales of crime as well as in pathetic stories of people innately good but struggling hopelessly against an unkind fate. Years elapsed before England realized that she was turning over to her expatriated citizens one of the best of her colonial possessions. Since then many of her worthiest sons and daughters have established homes there and today Australia is justly proud of her citizenry, her resources, and her culture. Two of the cities, Sydney and Melbourne, are approaching the million mark in population and are as modern and interesting as any cities of their size in the world.

Brother McKay, with every right-thinking Latter-day Saint, believes the acquisition of knowledge and proper experience is a duty. With this thought in mind he, in company with Brothers Cannon and Robert K. Bischoff, visited the famous Jenolan caves. No task could be more impossible of fulfillment than to adequately describe these wonderful formations, located far under the ground, the stalactites, the stalagmites, the dainty coloring, weird shapes, many of them seemingly the work of a master sculptor who had been called away before his task was completely finished.

The visitor is overwhelmed by the vastness, the uniqueness, and the sublime grandeur of countless chambers. There are exquisitely tinted curtains, transparent and looking as soft as the finest silk, delicately woven shawls, handkerchiefs, and draperies of fluffy lace which would win the ladies' hearts; there are flags and icicles and waterfalls; there are ferns and flowers, birds and animals, men and women. In one chamber the Madonna and Child are surrounded by glorified beings; in another are weird and grotesque figures which seem to belong to the nether regions. And all these are of stone made through forgotten ages by an omnipotent hand.

For untold centuries these marvels remained here, unknown, until an accident revealed the first of the caves to man. The thought comes to the visitor that all about are great and beautiful truths waiting for man's eyes to be opened so that they can be seen.

It required three hours to traverse the Orient cave, the most famous of the group, with its innumerable caverns. In doing so one must climb and descend fourteen hundred steps. In the bottom of this cave is an underground river which is crossed in a boat. All about were strange forms which were reflected by electric lights in the clear water, and the visitor feels indeed that he is in an enchanted fairyland.

Between the caves and the hotel, the travelers saw many rock wallabies, miniature kangaroos, somewhat larger than an ordinary rabbit, and which were almost as numerous and quite as tame as the sparrows in Utah.

Australia is typically English in at least one respect. Whether visiting famous caves, or traveling by auto or train, shopping or sightseeing, the traveler who does not have "Tea" every few hours is looked upon as a freak.

Several meetings were held in Sydney, after which a trip was made to Melbourne about six hundred miles distant. There a missionary meeting was held with the Elders. These brethren were working with energy and finding in their efforts that same spirit of sweet contentment so characteristic of faithful missionary work. There were present at these meetings President Milton Jensen and Elders Sterling Johnson, Thomas G. Smith, Franklin D. Fronk, Alvin Englestead, and John E. Hipwell.

From Melbourne Brother McKay and his party took a boat across Bass Strait to Tasmania, landing after an all night ride at the little town of Burnie and traveling 230 miles from that place to Hobart. On this island President Edward Eugene Gardner, Wallace O. Walker, Joseph L. Hunsaker, and James E. Hendricks were laboring. Hobart is one of the most southerly cities in the world, and one is forced to admire these young chaps who were working in this isolated field, seldom seeing missionaries other than their co-workers, and, because of the great distances, not being favored with frequent visits from the mission president. One can easily understand, therefore, how much they appreciated Brother McKay's visit. He not only gave them excellent instruction but delivered a message in the Town Hall which if obeyed will lead those who heard it back into the presence of the redeemed. In this instance also "some who came to scoff, remained to pray."

As the brethren were leaving Tasmania they were greeted at the wharf at Launceston by a number of members and friends. Among them was Brother Chidwick who celebrated his 81st birthday by seeing an Apostle for the first time. His joyful face bore evidence that it was one of the eventful days of his life.

After returning to Melbourne from Hobart, the special missionaries and President Rushton traveled to Adelaide, 483 miles distant. The Elders from the Melbourne district came down to the train to see the brethren off. They were a splendid looking lot physically, averaging better than six feet, and as they were standing by the train the conductor said in surprise, "My word! But it's unusual to see so many large men together." When Brother McKay told him they were all Mormon missionaries his astonishment was intensified.

The plan had been for the missionary party to go to Perth in western Australia, but it was found that the return to Sydney could not be made sufficiently early to catch the boat for Singapore, and the plan had to be abandoned. The Elders from Perth, therefore, came to Adelaide, a distance of 3,200 miles for the round trip, in order to receive the instructions which Brother McKay had to impart. There were in attendance at the missionary meeting Presidents Austin N. Tolman, and George A. Christensen and Elders Herman E. Bayliss, Earl R. Hansen, Thomas W. Lutz, Willaim C. Warner, Thomas G. Smith, and Sister Doris Baker, besides the visitors.

Attending the meetings held in Adelaide were some members who had come 200 miles to meet Brother McKay. They brought with them a hunger and thirst for the word of the Lord, and the promise made by the Savior to all such was completely fulfilled. All were unanimous in saying that a trip of many times the distance would have been small sacrifice for that which they received.

While looking for a suitable hotel at which to stay, the visitors had been thoroughly disgusted by the drinking and carousing in the public houses which were connected with every hotel. Following the English custom, barmaids served the drinks in these places. However, when the Sabbath came, the brethren were forced to admit that our own fair state could in some respects profitably follow the example of this land. Trams did not run until late in the afternoon, and the picture shows and all places of business were closed.

At the time of this visit, the Sunday School in Sydney was presided over by Brother J. N. Hansen. Before he joined the Church, he and his wife and little daughter went from Australia to Utah and located in the Thirty-First Ward, Salt Lake City. The wife was taken fatally ill and in his hour of greatest distress the family was visited by Relief Society sisters who aided him in every possible manner. His wife died, after telling him that the unexpected kindness had prompted her to ask the Lord whether Mormonism was divine or not. She bore solemn testimony just before she passed on that these principles were true and urged him to accept them. However, he was so disconsolate after her death that he returned to Australia, but later he sought and found the missionaries and he and his daughter became devoted members. Missionaries in foreign lands are not the only ones who preach the Gospel.

Another missionary meeting was held in Sydney attended by President and Sister Rushton, Elders Robert K. Bischoff, Sterling Johnson, Marion G. Romney, William W. Horne, William L. Jones, Robert H. Andrus, Raymond P. Nelson, Charles M. Bowen, Lorenzo F. Hansen, and the two visiting brethren.

Much has been said about the faithful services of the wives of mission presidents, and Sister Rushton was no whit behind her sisters in devotion. She had the love and confidence of Elders and members and was a worthy mother to her flock. The missionaries, too, laboring in this land measure up to those of any field visited as do also the members. Though they assist the missionaries in their zealous efforts to convert, it cannot be said that the work, judging by the number of baptisms, is making great headway in Australia.

If the sole purpose of the Church in sending representatives abroad were to win a large membership, the prospects in the Antipodes would be rather disheartening. Inasmuch, however, as its mission is to preach the "gospel of the kingdom . . . in all the world for a witness unto all nations" (Matthew 24:14), there is no cause for discouragement, and indeed those faithful ones, though few in number, who recognize the voice of a servant of the Lord are well worth all the effort expended in that land.

Before leaving Australia, indeed before steamship tickets could be purchased, it was necessary to have visas from the British officers to enter India and Egypt and from the Dutch officers to enter Java. These were not easily obtained. Nations had not yet reached a state of normalcy after the war and officials acted with the most exasperating deliberation. Under no circumstances could they be hurried. It appeared after all that the *Marella* might leave before the necessary papers could be obtained. But Brother McKay's principle is to go as far as he can, trusting in the Almighty to open the way further. He and President Rushton, therefore, went to Brisbane by rail, at which point the steamer was scheduled to call, leaving Brother Cannon to secure the papers and follow with the *Marella*.

Satan seemed determined to make this special mission as difficult as possible. Even more apparent, however, was the divine power, manifested so convincingly that the brethren knew they had but to proceed calmly and prayerfully with arrangements, no matter what apparently insurmountable obstacles might arise, and the way would be invariably opened. Had they hearkened to officials who assured them the papers could not possibly be prepared in time, their journey would have been seriously impeded.

Herein lies an important lesson which Brother McKay never failed to emphasize. "Even though a stone wall appears to cross your path," he was wont to say, "go as far as you can, and you will usually find an opening through which you can pass."

To illustrate this point, he related the experience of the late James L. McMurrin. Laboring as a missionary in Scotland, when a very young man, Brother McMurrin had been appointed to hold a meeting in a neighboring town, to which he must travel by train. He was penniless. The distance could not be traversed on foot in the time at his disposal. "I cannot go," he thought, "because of lack of means," but this was supplanted by a better thought, "I have been given this appointment and will go as far as possible and will only stop when I cannot go a step farther." He walked to the station and to the gate where he must show his ticket. Suddenly he met a friend who asked if he had any money and upon receiving a negative reply gave him enough for his railroad fare.

In no field visited was a better spirit manifested than in Brisbane, a flourishing town in Queensland in the northern part of Australia. The members, themselves joyful in their belief, are preaching the Gospel by word and by example.

The following Elders were laboring in this field: Oldroyd, Harold Q. Billings.

It was not easy for these good people to say good-bye to Brother McKay nor for the brethren to say good-bye to them. Many miles of land and water must be traversed before Church members would again be met. This was the last of the missions to be visited in the western hemisphere.

Another stop of twenty-four hours was made at Townsville, an industrious little town from which large quantities of meat are shipped. No missionary work was being done there. The brethren rode from the pier into the city in an old-fashioned carriage drawn by two spirited little horses. A few words of praise to the driver about his ponies prompted him to show what they could do; the result was that every horse-propelled vehicle on the road was passed. How pleasant are words of praise about something we love!

Naturally there was a decided change in temperature as the voyagers sailed in a northwesterly direction along the north coast of Australia, for here they were nearer the equator than they were while in Samoa. The vessel stopped nearly forty hours at Port Darwin, the most northerly of all Australian towns, and during this time the brethren witnessed a most interesting exhibition of native war dancing, put on for their special benefit. Having heard there was to be something of the kind given by the aboriginals, they walked out on a beautiful moonlit night into the country where these natives live. Their village consists of many small white cottages which in the moonlight seemed to be neat and well kept. People as black as coal were sitting in the doorways but took no notice of the visitors who walked through the entire village until they came to a great cliff overlooking the ocean. There they found a group of men and children and a few women, but the dance was over.

A young boy who spoke a little English was asked by Brother McKay what they would charge to put on a special exhibition.

"How many people do you want to take part?" asked the lad.

"All that are here."

"Would a shilling be too much?"

As there were about fifty people present, Brother McKay first thought the lad meant a shilling apiece, which would have been rather expensive, but he soon discovered that it was a shilling for the lot. The coin was immediately produced and another was promised if they gave a good performance.

Most of the men were completely naked and the combined clothing of those who were "dressed" could have been tied up in a pocket handkerchief. The dance was quite unlike anything the brethren had seen before, though it is something after the order of the "Haka" in New Zealand. It commenced by all slapping their bare thighs in unison. This became faster and faster. Then one of the men came forward from the group and danced with terrific speed, while the others continued the chanting and slapping with a uniform movement of the body. When the dancer was completely exhausted he retired and another took his place. It should be added that the women took no part in the exhibition.

The Commonwealth of Australia is made up of six states and one territory, which is under the control of the federal government much as our territories formerly were. They are: New South Wales, which is two and a half times as large as Great Britain and Ireland; Queensland, Victoria, Tasmania, the island lying to the south of the main continent; South Australia, Western Australia, and the Northern Territory. Their combined area is three million square miles, or about the same size as Europe. Australia has less than two inhabitants per square miles, while Java, which the brethren were to visit en route to Singapore, has six hundred.

One of the incomprehensible blunders of this enterprising nation is the condition of the railroads. Each state is the owner of its own system, and almost without exception it has a different gauge from all others. The result is that the traveler is compelled to change cars frequently when traveling from place to place. This is inconvenient. But when one remembers that freight must also be transferred, one realizes what a needless cost is involved. It is said that freight from Perth in the extreme west to Sydney has to be transferred four times before finally reaching its destination. Otherwise the train service is very tolerable and in some cases excellent.

Entrance to Jenolin Caves

CHAPTER 20

JAVA, SINGAPORE, AND RANGOON

"Prophecy is best proved in the light of its fulfillment."
— James E. Talmage

Australia's annual liquor bill amounts to many million pounds sterling. At the time of the visit herein described, the country was suffering from a shortage of water and officials were urging that it be used sparingly. One of the daily papers drily remarked that this was not intended to mean Australians could not drink what water they needed; and one of the reporters concluded, after making a trip which took him into many of the saloons, that most Australians felt they could not be loyal citizens and waste water by drinking it.

The tobacco bill must also be enormous. The man who does not smoke is rather a rarity and the women seem to be taking on this obnoxious habit with appalling rapidity. With the boat on which the brethren were traveling were many young people off on an excursion to India. With one exception they all smoked, both men and women. The exception was a very beautiful young lady, just the kind of a girl a man of middle age would be proud to claim as his daughter. She steadfastly refused the cigarette offered her by insistent friends until the night before Singapore was reached. The missionaries felt like shedding tears when they saw her weaken at the last moment and accept and smoke the proffered "coffin tack." It was a sad example of the danger of bad associates.

Some modernists find some difficulty in believing that prayers can be heard and answered. Such people would limit the Creator of the universe in his powers, though all are willing to admit that man, his creation, is unlimited. Here is an illustration of what men can do: These brethren were almost on the opposite side of the earth from their homes in Utah. One evening as the ship plowed through the waters of the Indian Ocean, Brother Cannon mentioned that on the following day his mother would be eighty-two years old. Brother McKay ordered him to send her a wireless message of love and congratulation. This was done, and as the good woman was eating her breakfast on the morning of her birthday the words which had traversed thousands of miles of land and water were delivered to her. In face of such wonders who will say the Almighty cannot hear the appeals of his children or even read the thoughts of their hearts?

The Dutch East Indies forms the largest cluster of islands known to man and is one of the world's most densely populated spots. Java, the most important island of the group, is about two thirds the size of Utah but has a population of between thirty and forty million people. Besides sustaining this great number it has a considerable amount of jungle in which the royal tiger, black panther, rhinoceros, wild boar, and other game are found.

There were people everywhere: bathing in rivers and canals, lying in the shade, squatting by the roadside, eating, drinking, smoking, a few pretending to work, but most of them doing nothing, everywhere as thick as ants. Indeed they would remind one of ants or bees in a hive, except that ants and bees are industrious.

Canals and rivers appear to play an important role in the country's daily life. From beds of streams much of the building sand is taken; they furnish a means for most of the transportation of the country, carry off the sewage and supply bathing places for man and beast. One might have said for women also, but as President Penrose used to say, man embraces the woman. The brethren saw a man scrubbing his oxen which had been driven into the stream. Not far away a woman was doing the family washing, while nearby another woman was washing her hair.

A barber shop in Java is unique. The barber goes about the town with a small stool and a little box containing his tools. When a customer is found the "shop" is set up in the shade and the desired shave or haircut is given. Restaurants partake of the itinerant character of the barber shop. The stock in trade and diminutive heater are moved about on wheels or the entire lot is divided into two loads and balanced in a basket on each end of a pole and carried Chinese fashion on the proprietor's shoulders.

At Sourabaya, the town next in importance to Batavia on the island of Java, the special missionaries were met by Frank W. Beecraft, of Ogden, who at the time was holding a responsible position with the Krain Sugar Company. Brother Beecraft was a former student of Brother McKay's, and far as known was the only Mormon among thirty million people. Though living in this isolated land and among a people with extremely low moral standards, his exemplary life did credit to parents, teacher, and Church. Having an auto at his disposal, he placed it and himself in the hands of his visitors and this kindness enabled them to see much that otherwise would have been missed. After driving about the city and surrounding country he took them out to the sugar mill. A part of the machinery in this factory was made in Provo, and an invention of Albert Genther, of Salt Lake City, was being installed.

Among the foreign population few nations are without representatives and even among the natives many distinct races are seen. Principal among these, besides the Javanese themselves, are the Sundanese, the Madurese, from adjacent islands, and the Malays from the Malay Peninsula. The Javanese homes are distinguishable from those of the other natives because they are built on the ground, whereas the others are built on poles in the air. There are no windows nor chimneys, and when cooking is done in the house the smoke must get out as best it can. However, fires are never made for heating and except in stormy weather the cooking is done outside.

The native food consists almost solely of rice and dried fish.

A very small plot of ground furnishes the one, and sea and river furnish the other. It is said that "to lack rice is to lack food." As for clothing, many of the men are "naked from the waist up and from the thighs down," though not infrequently trousers and even shirts are worn. The women with instinctive modesty are attired in "Mother Hubbards."

A stay of twelve hours in Batavia enabled the brethren to see Buitenzorg, the military and governmental headquarters of the Dutch East Indies. The Governor General's home is a veritable palace, as fine as that of any European king.

Scientists have said that in Java and Sumatra, a neighboring island, there is a greater degree of volcanic activity than anywhere else on earth. History records that Mt. Thunder in 1843 "during a slight eruption threw ten million tons of dust ten thousand feet high." One wonders what a severe eruption would do. At Batavia, from the 26th to the 29th of August, 1883, the sky was obscured, caused by the eruption of the Krakatau volcano on an adjoining island of this name. This has been described "as the greatest and loudest explosion ever recorded." It was distinctly heard in the Philippines and Japan, and even in Europe, though not so distinctly there. Forty thousand people were swept from one island by a great tidal wave following the eruption.

No organized missionary work has been done by this Church in Java. The low moral standard of the natives would make it difficult to obtain a foothold there. The whites temporarily residing in that land have gone with the idea of quickly enriching themselves, and consequently would hardly be inclined to study the Gospel seriously. Still there are doubtless many honest-hearted people in Java and at the proper time, the Church authorities will be inspired to open that populous field.

Forty hours of sailing from Batavia brings the traveler to the city of Singapore at the point of the Malay Peninsula. Approaching the harbor, the *Marella* was met by a veritable flotilla of frail canoes whose occupants begged the passengers to throw money into the water. When this was done it was interesting to see the skill displayed not only in diving for the coins but in climbing back into the skiffs without upsetting them.

Singapore lies directly north of the equator, but seven and one half degrees to be exact. It is of course extremely hot, and visitors are warned that they must either remain indoors during the day, or carry sunshades. The special missionaries, having neither sunshades nor any time to waste, ignored this advice, and managed to pull through.

Illustrative of how hot it is, one might mention that in hotels no provision is made for covers on the beds. One sleeps on sheets but not under them. By lying thus with all doors and windows open, and with a powerful electric fan playing upon him, the guest is able to obtain a fair night's rest. Of course the beds here, as in all tropical countries, are enveloped in a canopy of mosquito netting: a most necessary protection against insect pests.

It was late in the afternoon when the missionaries arrived at the hotel, and shortly thereafter they received a call from a Chinese tailor who solicited orders for linen suits, which he promised to have ready the following morning. Naturally everybody wears white clothing in the tropics, and being rather travel-stained, the brethren were in the market for something of this kind. Four linen suits were therefore ordered. Two of these were delivered the following morning at six o'clock and the other two before evening of the same day, at a cost for the four of about fifteen dollars.

It is claimed that more nationalities are represented in Singapore than in any other city of the world. And a few hours' stroll about the crowded streets rather substantiates this statement. After an evening walk the visitor is inclined to wonder what the houses are used for, impressed as he is with the thought that most of the inhabitants live on the streets. Men, women, and children are asleep in doorways, on window ledges, and on the sidewalks, which are also used for the numerous itinerant merchants, hucksters, and beggars.

Again difficulties were encountered in finding accommodations from Singapore on towards Calcutta. Brother Cannon was told that this would be impossible under two weeks, but during the afternoon arrangements were made to sail the next day with the *Bharata*.

The remarkable promise pronounced by President Lund upon the head of Brother Cannon that if he were ill it would be of very short duration had additional fulfillment here. En route from Singapore to Rangoon he was attacked by an excruciating pain. It was not a new experience, for several times in his life he had been similarly afflicted, and on all such occasions the pain had lasted for days. It was about two o'clock in the morning. He arose and went on deck. Naturally at that hour everything was quiet. Perspiration streamed from every pore, not because of the heat but due to intense suffering. When it seemed that this could not be longer endured, he called upon the Lord, and reminded him of the above mentioned promise. Instantly the pain vanished and did not return.

This experience is not related boastfully, but solely with the hope that it will increase faith in the hearts of the readers and as a humble testimony that the Lord lives and fulfills his every promise. The unbeliever will close his eyes to the miraculous healing, which was the fulfillment of an inspired prediction. He fails to see God's goodness. While in Australia these travelers met a faithful member of the Church, John Allen, who was completely blind. On one occasion this good man visited his brother-in-law, a pastor. Brother Allen bore testimony to the divinity of this work, to which the pastor replied, "John, you are blind; you cannot see." Brother Allen answered, "True I am physically blind, but your misfortune is greater than mine, for without eyes I can see the truth, while you are blind to that which is most precious in life."

Few cities in the world are more interesting than Rangoon in Burma. An incongruous mixture of wealth and squalor greets the eye. One passes rapidly from disgustingly filthy streets to beautiful avenues lined with stately residences and artistic gardens. The difference in individuals, too, offers quite as violent a contrast as do the streets. There were aesthetic and intelligent looking fellows with long hair, others with hair closely shaven except for one lock, similar to the scalping lock of the old time American Indian. Some men were gorgeously robed, while all about were those who wore nothing but ragged breech-clouts. And, judged by their faces and some conversations which were held, there is among them as wide a range of intellectual poverty and wealth, as is noticeable in physical appearance and temporal surroundings. Some of the beggars were revoltingly mutilated. The statement is reliably made that they disfigure themselves the better to appeal to a sympathetic public. The missionaries saw many groups of both sexes industriously hunting something smaller than elephants in each other's heads. They were left to guess what these hunters were seeking, but their guess was that they had better keep a safe distance from the groups—not an easy thing to do in the crowded condition of the streets.

The Shwe-Dagon is one of the noted buildings of the world. It is the first thing one sees on approaching Rangoon and the last thing upon which the gaze of the traveler lingers as the vessel moves down the muddy Rangoon river, a branch of the Irawadi, toward the sea. It was built many centuries ago as a Buddhist Temple, indeed its commencement dates back to 500 B.C. The great dome surmounting the building is covered with gold leaf, valued, according to the guide books, at about five million dollars. The pillars which support the various shrines are inlaid with glass mosaic which is not only beautiful but represents a vast amount of patient skill. In addition to the gold, there are 3,664 rubies, 541 emeralds, and 433 diamonds in this dome. The cost of other parts of the building is correspondingly great. Though the walks approaching and surrounding this impressive edifice were extremely dirty, the attention of the brethren was called to an illuminating sign, "Foot-wearing Prohibited." Before a curious crowd, therefore, they were obliged to turn up their trousers, unfasten garters and remove shoes and stockings. On either side of a long flight of steps leading to the court of this pagoda are open shops of all kinds. In one of these a man was trying to reach something from a high shelf. Not being tall enough and failing to see anything else on which to stand, he spoke to his wife, and she obediently lay down on her stomach, and by standing on her he was able to obtain the desired article. It was the first time the brethren had seen a woman used as a stepladder. Though the ground was too holy for the missionaries to walk on except with bare feet, men and women were smoking long black cigars of unusual thickness, and dogs and chickens added to the dirt.

One of the peculiar things about this place was the numerous professional prayer-makers. The visitor who desires a special blessing but who is too timid or ignorant to pray, may for a small gratuity, have one of these professionals do it for him.

The brethren were "On the Road to Mandalay," made famous by Kipling's verses, but they did not travel far thereon, as by good fortune they were able to exchange tickets on the *Bharata* for places on the *Arankola*, belonging to the same company, and which not only left Rangoon sooner, but was a much faster boat.

CHAPTER 21

INDIA

"But dost thou know what I would tell thee? In the primitive church the chalices were of wood, and the prelates of gold; in these days the church hath chalices of gold and prelates of wood."

— Girolamo Savonarola

Think of approaching India! Is there a well-read person in the world who has not desired to visit this densely populated and mystical land, with its ancient and almost forgotten civilization, its master builders long since dead, its bloody but absorbing history? To the westerner, eastern countries are full of incongruities, and no other land, Japan possibly excepted, has more surprises for the traveler than has India. One is inclined to think her primitive agricultural methods and her renowned buildings, which the most gifted pens have vainly attempted to describe, do not belong to the same race. Their farming methods awaken the thought in the visitor's mind that he is living in Adamic days; while white marble structures, surpassing anything else of the kind on earth, make him wonder if he has not been suddenly transplanted from this mundane to a celestial world, and is gazing on the palace of some heavenly king.

A globe-trotter, whom the brethren met in Japan, said that travelers should see India, then write FINIS across the bottom of the page, as there was nothing more worth seeing. Though his statement was extravagant, it was not without foundation. From the moment the missionaries left the muddy bay of Bengal, discolored for many miles by the turbid water of the Ganges and its numerous subdivisions, and entered the still muddier Hooghly, until they sailed from Bombay into the Arabian Sea, en route to Egypt, every hour is now a treasured memory. Their one regret was that a longer stay was impossible.

Who has not heard of the Ganges River, whose waters were formerly considered sacred, and still are to some extent? It has its source in the ice cave on the southern slope of the Himalayas and has a total length of more than 1500 miles. Its most important branch, the Hooghly, is navigable by large steamers as far as Calcutta, about 80 miles from the seaboard.

Many great thinkers have been born among this race. A number of England's outstanding men spent years in India: Clive, Hastings, Thackeray (who was born there), Macaulay, Roberts, Kitchener, and others. One can easily believe that their greatness is in considerable measure attributable to the habit of thought which was and to an extent is a predominating native characteristic.

Despite their vast numbers—almost a quarter of the earth's inhabitants—and the many splendid characters heretofore developed from this race, they are now considered incapable of self-government, and for years England has performed that duty for them. It reminds one of a puny man commanding a massive elephant, which has the potential power to crush its master, but is held in check by superior intelligence. A casual observance of the men would indicate that they are effeminate and physically weak, but in this respect appearances seem to be deceptive. The missionaries saw slightly built youths carrying trunks, which weighed at least 150 pounds, on their heads, and going up and down stairs with these burdens and with a satchel in each hand.

Few women are seen on the streets, and they usually have their faces covered. Indeed, it is not an exaggeration to say the women use nearly as much cloth to hide their faces as the men do for their entire covering, or as their European and American sisters do for a dress.

For ages the cow was looked upon in India as being sacred, and to this day more or less sanctity is attached to her. But with the ox it is different. His lot and that of the Asiatic buffalo is so hard, all the heavy work being assigned to them, that were they capable of thought they might anticipate the butcher's block as a paradise. The brethren had occasion to go into the largest bank in Calcutta, located on the city's most prominent corner. This institution was large enough that 125 clerks were visible, but directly before the entrance a cow was lying and peacefully chewing her cud, while pedestrians walked in the street rather than disturb her. In a city of more than a million inhabitants, this seemed to be giving the cow a rather prominent place.

Missionaries working in lands where fleas abound are wont to complain if they have one or two of these disturbing insects on them. But what would they think of this statement, for the truthfulness of which both the brethren will vouch: In their room in a hotel in Calcutta, partly stripped, they sat under electric fans, each with a basin of water. Brother Cannon caught and counted 157 fleas. Brother McKay did not count his, but insists that he found even a larger number. The effectiveness of these pests was materially lessened because the bodies and clothing of the brethren were so moist from perspiration, otherwise the torment would have been unendurable.

The traveler in India is obliged to carry his bedding with him. In a sleeping car he not only furnishes bedding but also makes his bed, unless he has a servant along, as of course most travelers have. However, missionaries do not have personal servants, so our brethren waited upon themselves, much to the surprise of fellow travelers and somewhat to their own embarrassment. When the train comes into a station a coolie asks for permission to sweep the car, for which service he expects a gratuity. No self-respecting servant in India would think of doing such work.

The motley throng of Arabs, Turks, Persians, Indians of many different tribes, and many other nationalities, all chattering like so many monkeys, made a scene at the Howrah station in Calcutta not soon to be forgotten. These people discuss a trivial matter, such as the time of departure or arrival of a train, and the way they shout and gesticulate makes one think a new revolution has commenced.

Inadvertently the missionaries took places in a compartment reserved for a gentleman and his two sons. Instead of resenting the intrusion, as Americans or Europeans would have done, these dark-skinned people showed true courtesy to the strangers, even offering to go themselves into another car. As soon as their mistake was discovered, the missionaries prepared to find another place, but the proper owners of the compartment politely but firmly insisted that they remain, and had their servants bring refreshments to the intruders. Truly a person seeking suggestions for self-improvement will find them everywhere. These gentlemen were true noblemen. As the sun went down their servant spread a rug before the window on the floor of the car and the father offered his evening prayer. First he knelt with folded hands. Then he raised hands to face, after which he knelt and twice touched the floor with his forehead. This same thing was repeated many times. When the father had finished, the older son went through the same ceremony, but the younger man declined, though repeatedly urged by his father to do so. Whether this was due to bashfulness in the presence of strangers, or to lack of faith, the missionaries were not to discover. The men impressed the observers as being deeply sincere and one had to admire them for performing a duty even though it might attract unfavorable attention. When the praying was finished they produced a pack of cards and the young man joined his father and brother readily enough in a game.

From the car windows the brethren saw many camels and occasionally an elephant feeding in the yards with domestic animals. Men and women were plowing with forked sticks, such as were used thousands of years ago, and with various contrivances were dipping water from the streams and pouring it into the thirsty soil.

Comparatively few people in Utah know anything about Agra, but all have heard of the renowned Taj Mahal, "A Dream in Marble." This structure is considered by travelers the most beautiful building in the world. Artists and poets have attempted to describe it, but these efforts fall so far short that no attempt will be made here, for the beauty of its architecture and the material of which it is composed, consisting of white marble adorned with precious stones, is indescribable.

The mature person who has not stood before things so beautiful that he has not known whether to kneel down and pray or sit down and cry, is deserving of pity. Such feelings come over the visitor to the Taj Mahal. With uncovered head, one stands in awe before it. If a word passed between Brothers McKay and Cannon during this visit, it was spoken in a whisper. There are many larger buildings in the world, but a faint idea as to the fineness of workmanship can be had when one remembers that 20,000 men worked 17 years in constructing it. It was built three centuries ago by the Emperor Jahan as a mausoleum for his beloved wife, and his own body now reposes in a marble casket by the side of that in which she rests.

Scarcely less beautiful, and no less interesting is the Fort, also located in Agra. One could see in imagination the gorgeously arrayed elephants carrying the royal party up the incline from the gates to the inner dwellings. The marble mosque was one of the finest things the brethren saw during all their travels. The queen's bedroom of marble, overlooking the Jumna River along the bank of which a caravan of camels moving in stately procession could be seen, must have gratified the taste of the most esthetic. Before the door of this bedroom is a marble basin, in which the queen took her rosewater bath. In another part was the harem, before which was a great marble bathing pool with seats around the sides for thirty-four ladies. Over each seat was a fountain, so if they preferred to sit and have the cool water pour over them instead of sporting in the basin, they could do so. Below was the prison where refractory members of the harem, who displeased their lord, were sent for punishment. Sometimes this was close confinement for hours, days, or even years. Not infrequently it was death, and the gallows is still there to which they were hanged by a silken rope.

The city of Agra is 792 miles from Calcutta, and Delhi is 115 miles farther inland. Brother McKay's purpose in traveling so far was to meet Brother John W. Currie, who lives at Srinigar, and other Church members. From letters, however, which were awaiting him at Delhi, it was learned that all members in India with the exception of Brother Currie, had left the Church and did not care to be visited. From his correspondence one judged Brother Currie to be a faithful member, but he wrote that due to the expected visit to Srinigar of the Viceroy of India and an official party, it would be impossible to obtain the necessary conveyance from Rawal Pindi, the end of the railway line, to his home, 200 miles distant. After a prayerful consideration of the subject it was decided that a delay of several weeks was not justifiable, in order to visit the one faithful Church member. Long letters were written to him, and preparations were made to sail from Bombay with the steamship *Egypt*.

Comparatively little missionary work has been done in India, though a few faithful men and women have joined the Church in that land. Many years ago two young sailors, members of the Church, were in Calcutta and left a tract at the garden gate of a very beautiful home. A servant was about to throw it away when the master asked for it. He was a doctor in the British Army and through this tract became a convert. Subsequently he went to Utah and was a devoted Church member during his remaining years. President George W. McCune of the Los Angeles Stake is one of his grandsons.

Delhi is the present capital of India, and the government offices of the country have been recently moved to this city from Calcutta. Though interesting and historical, with a fair share of noted buildings, one wonders why it should be the capital instead of Calcutta, which is much larger and more accessible to the outside world. Large ocean-going vessels can come to the former city, while it requires 24 hours with a fast train from the seacoast to reach the latter.

From Delhi the brethren traveled to Bombay nearly nine hundred miles and requiring 32 hours with a fast train. Bombay is beautiful and in many respects modern, though some of the sights it presents appear very strange to a westerner. For instance, a crowd of women were excavating a cellar. They carried the dirt out in baskets on their heads. It was slavish work, but every woman wore bracelets and earrings, most of them had nose rings, and a few had anklets and toe rings, and of coarse all were barefooted.

There are in India alone 220 million Hindus—more than the total number in the world belonging to the various Protestant religions. Christians are prone to look upon these people as heathens, but they often appear to be more devoted to their religion than are many who profess Christianity. And while this statement may offend some professed followers of the Savior, the Hindu is frequently, though by no means always, a more potent factor for righteousness in the lives of its adherents, than is modern Christianity. And why? Certainly not because its principles have more saving power, but because many Hindus believe more devoutly in their religion than do some Christians. It is a well-known and lamentable fact that an alarmingly large number of so-called Christians do not believe that Jesus Christ was actually the Son of God. They do not believe in his atoning death, nor in his literal resurrection.

The special missionaries discussed this point as they, aboard the *Egypt*, sailed out of the picturesque harbor of Bombay into the Arabian Sea, and expressed sincere gratitude for their testimony of his divinity, that he died for mankind and brought about the resurrection of the body. To them this testimony was priceless, more desirable than all the gold, silver, and precious stones of the earth.

On the ship was a pleasant and refined looking lady traveling with her three-month-old baby. The little one was fretful and the mother tired. Brother McKay, in the kindness of his heart, offered to relieve her by taking the child for a time. The mother feared it would not be good, but when he told her how many of his own he had lulled to sleep, she accepted the offer. He walked about the deck with the babe and soon it was fast asleep. One who saw it could not easily forget the look on his face when he brought the sleeping infant back to its mother and found her smoking a cigarette. Subsequently this woman was seen to nurse her baby and smoke at the same time.

Pyramid, Egypt

President Hugh J. Cannon and Elder David O.
McKay at Sphinx and Pyramids, Egypt

CHAPTER 22

EGYPT TO JERUSALEM

"Fear ye not, stand still, and see the salvation of the Lord, which he will shew to you to day."

—Exodus 14:13

Immediately after sailing from Bombay the brethren reached a point in the Arabian Sea which is exactly on the other side of the world from Utah. When it is six o'clock in the evening in Salt Lake it is six o'clock in the morning there. The first stop after leaving India was at Aden on the Arabian Peninsula, at the southerly end of the Red Sea. And of all the barren, desolate and unattractive places visited by these travelers, Aden was the most forbidding. Records show that it is no rare occurrence for two years to pass without a drop of rain falling, and the average rainfall is but a half an inch annually. The hills surrounding the city are as void of vegetation as is a paved street.

A stranger never lacks company in Aden. From the moment he steps out of the rowboat which has brought him from the vessel, anchored out in the harbor, until his departure, he is surrounded by a train of mendicants and peddlers, which, while robbing the trip of some of its pleasure, adds to its interest. These creatures can devise countless reasons why one should give them money. A young man about twenty years old deliberately put his bare foot in the way of one of the travelers. This action was observed in time to avoid stepping on it with full weight, but not soon enough to turn aside entirely. The whimpering fellow demanded compensation for what he claimed was a permanent injury and was noisily abetted by voluble sympathizers, though the ruse was so absurdly palpable. Of course he was not paid, but for a few moments a riot seemed inevitable.

From Aden our travelers entered the Red Sea and sailed 1,200 miles in traversing this body of water, which played such an important role in Biblical and Book of Mormon history. Often Arabia was visible on their right and Africa on their left. One of the peaks on the Arabian side was pointed out as Mount Sinai. However there is grave doubt as to whether or not this is the original Sinai, on which the ancient law was given.

In imagination one could see the intrepid Moses, so confident in the power of the Lord that the complaints of his followers were unnoticed, raising his staff with the command, "The Lord shall fight for you, and ye shall hold your peace" (Exodus 14:14).

It was also easy to see in fancy the small colony led by Lehi, whose trust in the Lord was as implicit as was that of Moses. He, too, remained as steadfast despite the grumblers, as did the other great leader.

M. de Lesseps, the French engineer, achieved a lasting name for himself by building the Suez Canal. As is generally known it extends from the Mediterranean to the Red Sea and is 95 miles long, and sufficiently wide for two large ocean liners by closely hugging the banks to pass each other. The country on either side is desolate, but its very barrenness is attractive. One feels the antiquity of the place. Not a blade of grass, not a tree or shrub or leaf was to be seen. One forms a slight idea of the barrenness of the country upon being told that when the 25,000 men engaged in building the canal had proceeded inland some distance, 1,500 camels were constantly required to carry drinking water to them.

The building of this canal was by no means a modern idea. In the fourteenth century B.C., an effort was made by Rameses II to construct such a waterway, and this was repeated at subsequent times. History records that one of these attempts made in the 7th century B.C. was abandoned after it had cost the lives of 125,000 men.

Brother McKay and his companion disembarked at Port Said, the point where the Suez joins the Mediterranean, and journeyed by rail to Cairo, passing through Zagazig on the way. Zagazig is said by students of Jewish history to be the place where the children of Israel maintained headquarters during the time of their captivity. Date palms, tall and stately and with their fruit hanging in great red clusters, were everywhere to be seen. When taken from the trees the dates neither look nor taste like the prepared product which one purchases on foreign markets.

Cows, oxen, and men were turning cumbrous, old-fashioned, but still effective waterwheels, which raised water from the streams and poured it over the arid land.

The Egyptians are fond of saying, "He who drinks from the Nile will come again." The thought is that water of this river, which exerts such a tremendous influence over their lives, has a subtle power of attraction. One might add without exaggeration, not the water alone but everything else in Egypt, the mosques, the pyramids, indeed the very atmosphere, and above all the history cast a fascinating spell over the visitor which makes him long to return to it.

When the Nile behaves properly, Egypt has "fat years." Otherwise they are sure to be most tragically "lean." The difference between normal low and high water averages something more than eight yards. Should it rise but slightly higher than this, great damage results; and if it fall but one yard short of its usual high water mark, a famine of greater or less severity ensues.

Cairo is a modern city of three-quarters of a million inhabitants, among whom Mohammedans largely predominate. Women of the better class are veiled, but less heavily than those of India. The city is noted for its mosques and artistic gardens. One may worship in a different mosque every day of the year, for there are more than 365 of them. The Nile runs through the city, and visitors are shown the spot where the babe Moses was left in care of his sister that he might escape Pharaoh's cruel edict.

One can travel the seven miles by streetcar, or auto, or on a camel from Cairo to the stupendous pyramids of Giza, which were built while the present race was still in swaddling clothes and which are rated even now as among the world's wonders. The road crosses the Nile and skirts the riverbank throughout this distance. It is a scenic and beautiful drive, lined on both sides for the greater part of the way with acacia trees.

As Brother McKay and his companion traveled along this road one morning before sunrise, they passed hundreds of donkeys and camels loaded with vegetables, fruits, and other supplies for the city's markets. Indeed, almost everything—coal, brick, building stone, and lumber—is carried on the backs of these patient beasts. One camel, frightened at an approaching automobile, broke away from its master and scattered its load as it went with surprising speed over the road.

To ride a camel is in itself a novel experience. The brethren engaged two of these animals to ride out to the pyramids. At a word of command from their driver they lie down while the riders mount; at another word they arise, cow like, on their hind legs first, and unless the rider exercises care he will be precipitated over the animal's head.

And then came the pyramids and the Sphinx! The visitor desires to be alone, but with the tormenting beggars in endless numbers, solitude is something to be craved but not enjoyed. Just at sunrise the brethren mounted the top of one of the pyramids, an exhausting bit of work, as there are no steps and one must climb from one high block of stone to another. But the view from the summit well repays the effort. Looking eastward one gazes upon the fertile Nile valley with its fields of corn, its majestic date palms, its vegetable gardens. In the distance the picturesque spires and minarets of Cairo glisten in the morning sun. To the north, west, and south is the Libyan desert as barren and devoid of vegetation as the Sahara.

One may read of the pyramids and see pictures of them, but to gain even a faint idea of their colossal proportions it is necessary to climb to the top of one of them. After doing so, one is prepared to believe that Cheops, the largest of the group, contains 2,300,000 blocks of stone which average three and a half tons in weight, and that 100,000 men worked in its erection three months in each year for twenty years.

The ancient Egyptians believed in a literal resurrection, but the resurrection depended largely on the preservation of the body after death; hence the remarkable skill displayed in mummifying bodies and the sacredness with which these were viewed. For this reason men of power and wealth built tombs in which their remains could be hidden. With what horror would they have looked into the future and seen these bodies dragged out of carefully prepared hiding places and exhibited in museums to the gaze of every curious visitor!

There are nine pyramids in this immediate vicinity, three large and six smaller ones. But they are not the only objects of interest. Indeed one is tempted to say they are less awe-inspiring than the inscrutable but majestic Sphinx, which scientists say was no longer young when Abraham visited Egypt thousands of years ago because of famine in his own land. It is hardly too much to say that more has been written about this figure than about any other one inanimate thing in the world. But it stands there silent and scornful, though part of its nose has been torn way by the bullets of vandals, incomparably greater than the sum total of all that has been said or written on the subject.

In the glory of a beautiful early morning, Cheops presents a majestic appearance. One approaches it with a feeling of deep solemnity. What does the mammoth thing mean and why was it erected? Was it built as an astronomical observatory, or that its sides should afford to posterity standards of measurement, or was it merely built as a tomb for one man, its builder? Is it a monumental prophecy foretelling the great events in the world's history but in a manner so obscure that only subsequent to its fulfillment is the prophecy recognized?

With camels and a guide the brethren rode from the pyramids of Giza to the ancient city of Memphis, passing en route the pyramids and tombs of Ti, near Sakhara. One of these pyramids is said to be the oldest structure in the world. Among these tombs is one where the bulls of Apis were buried, and with more pomp and ceremony than is usually accorded human beings, even of high rank, for these bulls were held sacred by the Egyptians. Not only were they buried in royal tombs, but their bodies were mummified as well.

How these monster sarcophagi, each one carved out of a massive block of stone, and capable of holding the mummy of a bull, could be lowered into the underground grotto is one of the mysteries. At the time of this visit twenty-four had already been discovered, and it was expected that many more would be found.

On this trip the brethren passed a wedding party, conveying the bride to the bridegroom's house where the marriage ceremony would be performed. This procession reminded the guide of his own experience which he related. The details of an Egyptian match are arranged by other parties, the first meeting of bride and groom usually being at the place appointed for the ceremony. Abdul had paid one hundred pounds sterling to the father of his first bride, but the girl was so homely and otherwise unsuitable, in his opinion, that he sent her back to her parents, and lost his money. Subsequently he decided to try again, and was told of a very beautiful girl, a real bargain at 150 pounds sterling. The recommendations appeared so genuine that he paid the required sum and invited a number of English tourists to the wedding to see the jewel he had won. What was his chagrin when he found this bride to be worse even than the other! One of the English ladies exclaimed:

"My goodness, Abdul! Is that your wife?"

"No," was his answer. "That's my brother's wife. I decided to postpone my wedding." This girl therefore went the way of the other—to her parents—and he again lost his money. Brother McKay told him how such things were managed in America, and Abdul concluded by saying, "There's some sense to that. We're a lot of bloody fools over here."

A fast train carries one from Cairo to Kantara, where the traveler bound for Palestine crosses the Suez Canal on a pontoon bridge. From there an excellent train with sleeping and dining cars can be taken direct to Jerusalem. The time consumed between the two capitals is about 15 hours.

On a world tour the traveler enters so many different countries that unconsciously he develops a marked degree of unconcern. But the "Holy City," the city of unnameable memories—no real Christian can approach it without being overwhelmed by feelings of deep reverence. David O. McKay, himself an Apostle and a special witness, and as sincere a believer in the divinity of Jesus Christ as any man who lives, was deeply moved, and his companion partook of the same spirit. To walk on ground once hallowed by the touch of the Savior's feet, to see the places where he lived and taught and suffered and finally performed the noblest act ever witnessed by mortal man is an inspiration to every true believer.

A gifted writer might perhaps describe imperfectly what one sees in Palestine. What one feels is wholly indescribable, and must be left to the imagination.

After traveling for miles over a level plain, the train puffed slowly through ravines and narrow valleys, terraced and planted with grape vines, up the somewhat steep grade to Jerusalem, which is 2,900 feet above the Mediterranean. The surrounding hills are composed largely of white limestone and chalk formations and in the glaring sunlight of the east, these with the white buildings make a sight that is decidedly dazzling. The city is a natural fortress being almost entirely surrounded by a valley three or four hundred feet deep. But despite its natural advantages Jerusalem has been captured and re-captured oftener perhaps than any other city in the world.

Count Eberhardt, a German writer, is credited with the saying: "There are three acts in a man's life, which no one ought either to advise another to do or not to do; the first is to contract matrimony, the second is to go to the wars, and the third is to visit the Holy Sepulcher. I say that these acts are good in themselves, but they may easily turn out ill, and when this is so, he who gave the advice comes to be blamed as if he were the cause of its turning out ill."

The significance of this statement can be appreciated after a visit to Bethlehem, Calvary, and the Holy Sepulcher. Most Christians, regardless of church affiliations, who visit these places join in the wish that they had been left as they were anciently, instead of having been ornamented by altars, crosses, and churches, all of which are profusely adorned with gold and silver. In the church now standing on Calvary is an immense cross, and over it the inscription in letters of diamonds, "Jesus, King of the Jews." Nearby is a cabinet which contains, so our missionaries were told, treasures of gold, silver, and precious stones worth more than ten million pounds sterling. So interested are the guides and the average tourist in this gaudy display that nothing is said or thought of what the original cross cost in human suffering. One hears much of perishable worldly treasures, but the value of imperishable Christianity is unmentioned.

This thought also comes to the visitor: Suppose an expert but dishonest jeweler should chip out the real gems and pure metals and replace them with glittering substitutes. Might not this counterfeit pass, undetected by the masses, until perchance the original builder came along? The spurious might closely resemble the genuine, yet his trained eye would at once note the deception, and he would expose the fraud. Then suppose the populace should exclaim indignantly: "There has been no substitution. These treasures as they are were accepted by our parents and they are good enough for us." Would not Calvary and its surroundings greatly resemble the present condition of Christianity?

CHAPTER 23

PALESTINE AND SYRIA

"Or is it to be certain that my piece of bread belongs only to me when I know that everyone else has a share, and that no one starves while I eat?"

— Count Leon N. Tolstoi

Sweet yet solemn thoughts enter the traveler's mind while journeying to Bethlehem, passing on the way from Jerusalem the "fields of the shepherds," where these men "watched their flocks by night" and where they reverently and in awed wonderment listened to the heavenly choir as it sang, "Peace on earth, good will to men."

Bethlehem has about eight thousand inhabitants, most of whom profess to be Christians. Over the spot where the holy manger stood, a church built by the Emperor Constantine now stands. The Greek Catholics, Roman Catholics, and Armenians own the structure jointly, though each denomination must keep within its own boundaries. Under one roof, all worship (with their lips) the Prince of Peace, and hate each other so bitterly that a fight ensues if one of opposite faith dare cross the boundary line. A quarter of a century ago the Armenian Christians, who have but a small corner of the place for their altar, permitted a carpet to be moved beyond their rightful limits, while the floor was being swept. The consequence was a fight in which three men were killed. Pictures hang on the joint entrance hall so completely covered with dust that their outlines are not discernible, but no one dares touch them because of the jealousy of the other owners.

The silver and gold with which this sacred spot is decorated seem more of a desecration than an adornment. How could one think of beautifying the simple manger where the Son of God was born! Worldly treasures in this holy place are like the fantastic tales with which imaginative writers have attempted to color and make more beautiful the days of his babyhood.

Overwhelmed by a spirit of sadness, the visitor leaves, one by one, the Church of the Nativity, the place of the Crucifixion, and the Holy Sepulcher, wondering whether Count Eberhardt was not right in saying one ought not to advise another to visit this place. A feeble and uncertain faith might easily be destroyed by an exhibition of the hatred which professed believers in the Nazarene have one for another.

Various denominational structures have been erected on the Mount of Olives, and although many people were about, including groups of women engaged in picking the olives which were just ripening, it was possible for our missionaries to find a quiet spot where they could commune with the Lord. They had abundant reason to be thankful that their lives had been spared, that the prophetic promise made them had been fulfilled, and for the privilege of visiting this land.

They thanked him for the work of redemption wrought by his Son and for the restoration of his saving plan. They invoked his blessing upon the Church and its members in their gathered and scattered condition, for all the honest in heart, and they besought the Almighty to remember the city and country lying at their feet, that the Jews might be returned to the land of their fathers in fulfillment of ancient and modern prophecies.

It was an impressive occasion. The veil separating the brethren from the presence of the Lord seemed very thin. Below them was what is known as Stephen's Gate, for here the first martyr, after the Savior, gave his life for his testimony. These missionaries do not claim to have seen, as Stephen did, the heavens open and the Son sitting on the right hand of the Father, but they knew no less certainly of the existence of these Beings.

It is about fifteen miles in a straight line through the hills of Judea from Jerusalem to the Jordan and the Dead Sea. It is twenty-one miles by the road which, after passing Stephen's Gate, the Garden of Gethsemane, the home of Mary, Martha, and Lazarus in Bethany, winds about the base of the Mount of Olives. Standing on the bank of the Dead Sea the visitor is on the lowest part of the earth's surface not covered by water. Engineers have figured that the surface of this "Sea of the Plain" is 1,308 feet below sea level. The valley of the Jordan for the most part is uncultivated, but the high brush which covers it indicates fertility. Water and cultivation will make it once more blossom as the rose.

The Jordan, Jericho, Elisha's Fountain, Mount Temptation, and innumerable other historic points are deserving of mention but space will not permit.

Within the limits of Jerusalem are several hills. Next in point of interest perhaps to Calvary is Mount Moriah. Its history dates back to the memorable occasion when Abraham came to it with his young son Isaac. Later the great temple of Solomon was erected here. This was destroyed with the rest of the city as foretold by the Savior. Since then possession of the spot has passed to the Mohammedans, and now the great Mosque of Omar stands on the sacred hill.

There are few streets in Jerusalem which will accommodate a vehicle of any kind. They are narrow and evil-smelling, crowded with people and donkeys, and are ideal breeding places for all kinds of vermin.

The special missionaries were in Jerusalem on November 2, 1921. On that date every shop in the city was closed and the people indulged in such serous rioting that British soldiers were called into action and armored trucks carrying machine guns were stationed about the city. The trouble started as a protest against the declaration of Lord Balfour of England, that Palestine should be set apart for the Jews. By this declaration, the British statesman set in motion, to a far greater extent than he imagined, the fulfillment of prophecy, for not only do the Bible and the Book of Mormon foretell such a gathering of the Jews, but a modern prophet, Orson Hyde, one of the Twelve, predicted that England would play a leading part in this gathering.

Mohammedans and Christians, united in their hatred of the Jews if on no other point, stoned these unfortunates in the streets, and naturally where their numbers warranted it, the Jews retaliated. At one place Brother McKay, in righteous wrath, ordered a number of Christians to desist in the assault upon some helpless Jewish women and children, and with such sternness that the offenders were convinced he would, if necessary, follow his orders with physical force. The missionaries made an excursion into the Jewish district where they found frightened but sullen and defiant people. An hour or so later in that same street a bomb was thrown which killed a number of Jews and injured many more. At five o'clock in the afternoon everybody was ordered off the streets and heavily armed British soldiers and armored trucks with machine guns soon thereafter restored order.

The guide, professedly a devout Christian, who showed the brethren about, but only through the quiet streets, said that blood would flow before the Jews would be permitted to return to Jerusalem. However, they were convinced from the man's timidity that he will shed no blood; and if anyone sheds his, it will be because they can outrun him.

The following is a note taken from Brother McKay's journal: "I have not been disappointed in my visit to old Jerusalem. Its picturesque site on the four historic and frequently mentioned mounts, with its relative position to other Biblical centers, has been so clearly impressed upon my mind that this geographical significance itself is quite a sufficient reward for the journey. Besides this, the trip from Jerusalem to Jericho and the valley of the Jordan, with all their Biblical associations, was so full of interest and instruction that, were there nothing else, I should feel satisfied.

"No, I am not disappointed but grieved: grieved to see the manger, the sacred cradle, profaned by the ostentatious spirit of the jarring selfish creeds: grieved to see the spot desecrated by lavish wealth: grieved to learn of the feuds and quarrels that have occurred upon the very spot where the Son of God was born: grieved to see the keys of the Holy Sepulcher kept by a follower of Mohammed because the professed Christians cannot trust one of their number with them! Grieved to witness the same so-called Christians uniting with Mohammedans in opposing the return of the Jews to the Holy Land!

"How far, oh how far from the simple principles of the Gospel have they wandered who now profess to be the direct descendants of the primitive church! Greeks and Romans both are completely apostatized, and the very sects of Protestantism, of course, are ever wandering in darkness because they have no authority."

The reader may remember that Brother McKay's party returned to Utah after having been in China and Japan. Prior to leaving Salt Lake the second time, President Grant suggested it might be advisable to have someone who had labored in Syria meet these special missionaries and assist in distributing the money which had been collected for the suffering Armenian Saints. This suggestion was welcomed by Brother McKay, but nothing definite was decided at the time of leaving.

In Cairo word was received that Joseph Wilford Booth, who was the last missionary to labor in Syria and the surrounding country, had again been called to that land, and had already left for his mission. In the prayer offered on the Mount of Olives, already referred to, the Lord was asked so to direct the brethren that they might meet Brother Booth. He understood the language and the needs of the people, and it seemed imperative that they find and cooperate with him.

Brother McKay had planned to leave Jerusalem by auto, traveling through Samaria. However, after descending from the Mount of Olives, the brethren were united in feeling they should go by rail to Haifa, on the Mediterranean coast and immediately below Mount Carmel, which is remembered especially as the place of contest between Elijah and the prophets of Baal as recorded in

1 Kings 18, and which resulted so disastrously for those who had without warrant assumed divine authority.

It should be remembered that Brother McKay had left Salt Lake on the 26th of March traveling west, and Brother Booth on September 16th traveling east. Neither party was informed as to the whereabouts of the other. Indeed, Brother McKay had just learned that Brother Booth had been called, and for all the latter knew Brother McKay might still have been in Australia or India or might even have passed Palestine en route home.

Usually before these special missionaries entered a city, they made inquiries as to the name of a suitable hotel, but in this instance it was not done, though the brethren intended doing it, and spoke of it more than once. Ignorant of where they were to go, a delay of a few moments ensued in the station at Haifa, and as they were finally leaving, a man suddenly rushed up with an exclamation, "Isn't this Brother McKay?"

The inquirer was Brother Booth. Leaving Utah nearly six months later than the others and traveling in the opposite direction, he had met them exactly at the spot where it was absolutely necessary for them to meet in order properly to perform their work. Had they not met at Haifa, it is doubtful whether they would have done so at all, for Brother McKay's intention was to go to Damascus, while Brother Booth planned to proceed to Beirut. His passport entitled him to go to this point and no further. This fortunate meeting, apparently the result of chance, and in which the skeptic would admit nothing but a remarkable coincidence, was due to divine intervention in answer to prayer; and the three missionaries gratefully acknowledged the Omnipotent hand in it.

Because of letters which Brother McKay carried from the Secretary of State in Washington, the Consul in Beirut approved of Brother Booth's going further into Syria, and while he could not guarantee the protection of the United States, he did promise that if any trouble occurred with the officials or with lone bandits, he would use all the power of his office to give relief.

It was necessary to make the journey of about 80 miles from

Haifa to Beirut by auto. The road for almost the entire distance runs along the scenic coast of the Mediterranean and passed through the old and historic cities of Tyre and Sidon.

The route followed after their business in Beirut was completed led the brethren over the mountains of Lebanon to the city of Baalbeck. From these mountains Solomon obtained cedars for the great temple at Jerusalem. The hills are now entirely denuded, no trace of the trees for which they were once so famous being visible.

The origin of Baalbeck is unknown, though ample evidence exists of its great antiquity. Ancient writers describe it as being one of the finest of Syrian cities, beautified with fountains, gardens, palaces, and monuments. These have passed with the years, but the ruins of a series of temples, among them the Circular Temple and the Temple of the Sun, which must have been one of the greatest of the world, still remain. In one of the walls, which is still standing intact, are three great blocks of stone of such extraordinary size that one wonders what methods of building the ancients had, which would enable them to raise such massive stones and mortice them so exactly in a wall. In viewing these time-worn structures, one concludes that the thousands of intervening years have brought but little progress in the builders' art.

Brother McKay's party, now augmented by President Booth, were not long in Aleppo before realizing how helpless they would have been without the last-named brother; for the others did not understand the language, nor the conditions, and their visit would have been almost in vain. Being well acquainted in the city, and with many business men, Brother Booth soon located a member of the Church and in a few hours was in touch with all of them.

On the ship between Bombay and Port Said the brethren became rather well acquainted with General Frazier of the British army, who had spent many years in the Holy Land and the surrounding country, and who was looked upon as an authority on conditions there. He said to Brother McKay: "Unless you are prepared to leave your head behind, you should not go to Aintab."

This opinion was apparently shared by all consuls with whom the brethren talked. The most encouraging word they heard came from the British representative, who was met in the offices of the American consul in Aleppo. He said: "Oh, you may get through all right. The Turkish brigands are swooping down on the road every day or two, and robbing and in some cases murdering travelers, but if you happen to choose a lucky day you may have no trouble."

In describing dangers through which they passed, there is no desire to make heroes of these missionaries. Brother McKay is known as a fearless man, but his calmness and that of his companions was due not so much to courage as it was to faith, a faith which transcends courage. The prophet of the Lord had said to Brother McKay that he should be able to avoid dangers, seen and unseen, and in this promise the three brethren had sublime faith. All they had seen in recent days reminded them of that sermon: brevity and content considered, the most wonderful delivered since the beginning of time: "Fear not, only believe." To have doubted would, they felt sure, have been an insult to God.

It is 80 miles from Aleppo to Aintab, and with no railroad connection. This trip, therefore, had to be made by auto. It was arranged to leave one afternoon, but the spirit of the Lord indicated that they should not go, though their baggage was already in the car when Brother McKay decided to postpone the trip. Next morning it was different. All were eager for the journey, and though their driver was manifestly nervous, he alone was thus affected. Other autos were on the road, and one noticed a disposition on the part of drivers to keep close together as a matter of mutual protection, but the trip was made without interruption. Many wrecked cars were seen whose occupants had been robbed and the cars burned.

So uneventful was this journey that the missionaries might easily have felt the reports of danger were greatly overdrawn, but if such feelings existed they were dispelled when it was learned that the very day they passed over this road a company of people traveling with carriages and wagons was held up and robbed of everything worth carrying away, including sixty horses. No lives were reported lost, but these unfortunates were left, helpless, with vehicles but with no means of propelling them.

One cannot conceive of more heart-rending stories than those to which the brethren listened from the Saints in Aintab. Having suffered for food and shelter, they clung to the visiting brethren as they would to angels from heaven. Not a person was present but had lost some relative at the hands of the merciless Turks. One mother, with tears streaming down her cheeks, told of having become separated from her husband and three-year-old daughter in one of the raids made upon them. Later she learned of her husband's violent death, but had never heard a word from her babe and did not know whether it was alive or dead.

The money being distributed by these missionaries was raised for this purpose by a special fast day held in all stakes of the Church. It is not too much to say that every man or woman or child in Utah who fasted on that occasion would be willing to abstain from food for a week, or longer if necessary, could they have seen the good which their money was doing. Before Brother McKay left Syria, arrangements had been made to transplant all our members from the danger zone to Aleppo or Beirut where their lives at least would be safe, and where opportunities could be created for them to earn a livelihood. No man in the Church is better qualified than is Brother Booth to carry out this work. Though these events occurred more than six years ago, he is still in that land laboring unselfishly and with zeal. This good man loves the Lord and his fellowmen with all his big generous heart and is willing to spend his mortal life in the service. It may be interesting to our readers to know that he is a brother of Sister Mav Booth Talmage, wife of Dr. James E. Talmage of the Quorum of Twelve.

It was not easy to say good-bye to him and leave him alone in Aleppo. His family was in Utah and he had no missionary companions. And still he was not alone, for few men have more of the companionship of the Holy Spirit than does he. Since this visit was made his wife has been called to labor with him.

Meeting Wilford Booth at Railroad Station near Haifa

CHAPTER 24

HOMEWARD BOUND

"So it's home again, and home again, America for me!
My heart is turning home again, and there I long to be,
In the land of youth and freedom beyond the ocean
bars,
Where the air is full of sunlight and the flag is full of
stars!"

—Hnery Van Dyke

En route from Aleppo to Haifa the brethren visited Damascus. This city, according to many authorities, is the oldest in the world, and all concede that it is one of the oldest. Towards this place Saul of Tarsus was journeying "yet breathing out threatenings and slaughter against the disciples of the Lord" (Act 9:1) when he saw the light which resulted in his complete conversion. The street called "Straight" is still one of the most interesting thoroughfares in this ancient city. It is little more than four yards wide and the pedestrian is jostled not only by fellowmen, but also by camels and donkeys.

Along this street Ananias came, responsive to the Lord's command, and found Saul, humble and blind since the wondrous vision. One might suppose that a "chosen vessel" who had talked with the Lord needed nothing more, but Paul, as the Savior, had to obey the law of God, so he was baptized. The house where this meeting occurred still stands as does also that of Ananias, where, tradition says, Paul lived for some time while he sought to undo the harm he had formerly done. In another building one may see the window from which friends of the zealous convert lowered him over the wall in a basket, that he might escape his watchful enemies.

The Barada river flows through Damascus and is one of the really attractive things about the city. This river, the Abana of the Bible, is the stream of which the great Syrian captain spoke so boastfully when commanded by the Prophet to dip seven times in the waters of Jordan, "Are not Abana and Pharpar, rivers of Damascus, better than all the waters of Israel? may I not wash in them, and be clean?" (2 Kings 5:12.)

The brethren were in Damascus on the birthday of Mohammed, and as most of the city's inhabitants belong to his faith, it was a great holiday. Buildings and even sidewalks were adorned with various draperies, among them being some very ornate and costly Turkish rugs. The people were all arrayed in festive attire. In Paul's day but few Christians were in Damascus, and if one may judge from a brief and superficial observation, there are even fewer today who really believe in and follow the teachings of the Savior.

Together with other travelers, the brethren took auto from Damascus over the mountains of Lebanon to Beirut and from there again through ancient Tyre and Sidon to Haifa. Tyre and Sidon themselves are old-fashioned, with narrow, crooked, and in most cases dirty streets, but they occupy attractive sites on the shore of the Mediterranean, and in spite of dirt and beggars invite a longer stay.

In this day of high speed, it is not easy to realize how small the territory was to which the Savior's earthly ministry was limited. In two days, without undue loitering, one may drive by auto from Jerusalem to Bethany, Jericho, the Dead Sea, through the Jordan valley, around the Lake of Galilee, Tiberias, Cana, Nazareth, and back to Jerusalem through Samaria, visiting practically every place honored by a mortal visit from our Lord.

And yet one feels after a few weeks' stay that many long years would be insufficient to absorb and properly digest all that should be learned in this land. Every spot has a history. Here is the cave near the brook Cherith in which the prophet Elijah lived when raven brought him bread and flesh morning and evening. There is the spot where he stood, in company with Elisha, and divided the water of Jordan by smiting it with his mantle. Yonder is the field where the child which was given the Shunammite woman as a son of promise was stricken with illness, and farther on is the probable spot where the parents lived and where the little one was restored through divine favor.

Yon somber towering peak is Mount Temptation where tradition says the Savior was tempted of Satan. Over there John was preaching repentance when Christ came to him demanding baptism. Into this stream they went and the Son of God was buried in water by one having authority "to fulfil all righteousness." From the opened heavens the Father thus acknowledged this act of obedience, "This is my beloved Son, in whom I am well pleased" (see Matthew 3:15, 17).

To the north is Nazareth, Christ's boyhood home. The well, still known as the Virgin's well and from which, following the ancient custom, the boy and his mother doubtless carried water for the household use, is to be seen. Nearby is the rocky promontory from which his angry townsmen proposed to throw him after his first sermon in their midst. Between Nazareth and Tiberias stands the village of Cana, scene of the first miracle, the changing of water to wine.

And Galilee! The very name is inspiring. Gazing upon its blue surface, one need not be strongly imaginative to see a picture of the living Christ, healing the sick, casting out unclean spirits, giving sight to the blind, stilling the storm, walking on the water, even raising the dead. One remembers how he, with perfect knowledge of nature's laws, created from surrounding elements sufficient food to satisfy the multitude.

There is not complete agreement among Bible students as to the mountain on which the transfiguration occurred or on which the beatitudes were given; but undoubtedly both are in the vicinity.

It is not easy to describe the contradictions which confront the traveler in the Holy Land. Uplifted by the sacred truths which have been taught, he feels his own life enriched by contemplating the lives of those inspired teachers. But he sorrows in the glaring evidences of apostasy wherein professed followers of the Nazarene have "a form of godliness, but ... deny the power thereof." (Joseph Smith—History 1:19.)

The last evening of their stay in Palestine was spent by the missionaries on Mount Carmel. It requires about one hour of good walking to reach the summit. Here a stone marks the supposed place where the prophet Elijah called down fire from heaven. From this point the beauty of the surrounding scene is indescribable. The moon had just risen over the peaceful waters of the Mediterranean, and the lights from steamers and boats twinkled in the harbor. In the opposite direction one could look into the valley of the Esdraelon and almost into that of the Jordan. At the foot of the mountain was the quaint city of Haifa. It was a fitting place and hour to bid farewell to the country toward which the hearts of all Christians naturally turn.

Long before daylight next morning the brethren left by rail for Egypt. They again crossed the Suez at Kantara. Two days later aboard the *Ormonde* they were steaming across the Mediterranean toward Italy.

In Utah one thinks of Europe as being far away, but now after all their journeyings it seemed that they were coming into the borders of their own land.

Between Port Said and Naples they passed Fair Havens on the small island of Crete where the Apostle Paul, then a prophetic prisoner en route to Rome, entreated the centurion to put up for the winter. "Nevertheless the centurion believed the master and the owner of the ship, more than those things which were spoken by Paul" (Acts 27:11). Failing to heed the inspired words, the captain after severe buffeting by wind and wave, saw his vessel wrecked and its passengers cast upon the little island of Melita, barely escaping with their lives. Melita was also visible from the *Ormonde*'s deck.

A short time after passing those islands the brethren sailed between the real, not metaphorical, Scylla and Charybdis, so renowned in ancient story. Scylla is a dangerous rock on the Italian coast, and Charybdis a whirlpool on the coast of Sicily, a short distance away. This narrow passage seems to have lost its terrors for mariners; the *Ormonde* entered it just after nightfall, when by hurrying it might have passed through by daylight.

The bay of Naples is considered the most beautiful in Europe. On the starboard side as the vessel steamed into harbor, dense clouds of smoke were issuing from temperamental Vesuvius, and this was reddened from time to time by a fiery glare from seething lava within. On their port side was Naples, very attractive in the early morning light. All about were rowboats whose occupants were out early in the hope of obtaining money. Many of them offered fruits and flowers; some were following the Pacific Islanders' custom of diving for coins; a quintet was furnishing music and of a better quality than is usually heard under such circumstances; not a few were unvarnished beggars who made no pretense of offering anything in return for what they received.

Vesuvius, though greater because of past achievements than for its present power, has by no means reached a condition of senility; and the constant rumbling reminds the spectator who peers over the side that it may again break out and bury under molten ashes all surrounding regions. Pompeii, of course, is a stern reminder of what this volcano can do in a destructive mood. One cannot gaze into this molten pit without realizing what tremendous power lies in the forces of nature, and how utterly dependent man is upon the Almighty. Remove his controlling hand but for a moment and think what havoc would be wrought by wind, water, and fire!

The thoughtful Christian's heart is peculiarly stirred upon seeing Rome, with its numerous and costly churches, especially after visiting the Holy Land and being impressed with the manner in which the Gospel was formerly taught. On the one hand was simplicity, humility, self-sacrifice, where the greatest was "the servant of all." On the other, one sees pompous pride, men haughtily holding out hands to be kissed, mysterious ceremonies, and the poor and downtrodden of the earth shout out from the presence of the so-called representatives of the loving Christ. What has Rome done for Christianity? The answers would be as varied as the religious complexions of those giving them.

Now fallen into disuse and partially in ruins is the great Coliseum. Here gladiators fought with each other or with animals, and here, too, defenseless Christians, men, women and even little children, were torn to pieces by wild animals rather than abandon faith in their Redeemer, while more than fifty thousand spectators, no less cruel than the ferocious beasts, taunted victims and gloated over their death. It is interesting to know that this great structure was completed by Titus, the Roman general who destroyed Jerusalem according to the predictions of the Savior, something less than four decades after the prophecy was uttered.

It is supposed that both Peter and Paul met death in Rome, the former by crucifixion and the latter by being beheaded. Now two great churches stand on the supposed sites of the martyrdom and bear the names of the two Apostles. One wonders why, after centuries of teaching, the world still persists in deifying dead prophets and apostles and rejecting and in some cases killing the living ones.

Among the most interesting sights of Rome are the Catacombs, great subterranean rooms and passageways where, during the cruel persecution of the early Christians, they held meetings and frequently lived in hiding to escape the searching soldiers. The careful observer can trace in these underground galleries signs of departure from the simple Christian faith and in its place the introduction of ceremonies which were so inseparable from the Roman worship of their idolatrous gods.

Viewing these things the Latter-day Saint is grateful for the simplicity of his faith, so free from ostentation and all that is mysterious, its sole adornment being the "beauty of Godliness."

Brother McKay's oldest son, David Lawrence, was laboring as a missionary in Lausanne, Switzerland, and naturally it was planned to visit him in his field of labor. The young man was anxiously waiting the train's arrival at midnight, though he had little reason to expect his father, as the telegram which was sent had not been delivered.

Young Brother McKay is a worthy son and loves his parents with a deep and sincere affection. If no other reward were ever to come to him for his devotion to this work, he would be repaid in the pride and joy written on his father's face as they sprang into each other's arms. It reminded one that some day we will all meet our Heavenly Father. Will he joyfully greet us with open arms, and will we be able to hold our heads erect and look fearlessly into his searching eyes?

This may be an opportune place to mention a lesson which Brother Cannon learned during this trip. As was natural, Brother McKay always prayed for his missionary son in the joint petitions which he and his companion offered each day. Brother Cannon fell into the habit, when asked to be mouth, of mentioning Lawrence by name. He soon came to love the young man dearly, though prior to the meeting in Lausanne they were not acquainted. He learned that we love those for whom we sincerely pray. To follow Christ's example we must love our enemies; therefore we must pray for them. To be guided by the authorities of the church we must love them; therefore we must pray for them also. And for the same reason we should pray for all mankind.

An interesting conference was held at Lausanne under the direction of President Serge F. Ballif of the Swiss and German Mission, who translated the remarks of the visitors into French. The special missionaries had not met with Saints for several weeks, and they rejoiced in the spirit which is so characteristic of such meetings. In addition to young Brother McKay, other Elders were met in Lausanne.

There is something sadly lacking in the man who, after spending months in foreign lands and among strange peoples, can turn his face homeward without being thrilled to the depths of his soul. To think of one's native land, of home, of wife and children and other dear ones makes the thoughtful and appreciative man praise God. With the departure from Palestine, Brother McKay felt that the work for which he was especially called had been accomplished, and desired to return as soon as possible. Christmas was approaching and by hurrying the brethren could spend this blessed day with their families. Merely the high points, therefore, in the journey from Port Said to Utah are touched.

A brief but very pleasant visit with President Serge F. Ballif and his wife and daughter was made in the Mission Home in Basel, and a crowded meeting was held there. Brother Max Zimmer translated for Brother McKay while Brother Cannon struggled through his address without help. And it was a struggle, for more than sixteen years had elapsed since he left the Swiss and German Mission, and during that period he had used the language but rarely.

At Frankfurt am/Main a crowded meeting was held. Here Brother Jean Wunderlich, then a boy in high school, made his first attempt at public translating from English into German and acquitted himself most creditably. Since then he has translated for at least five of the Twelve.

Time did not permit of a trip by boat down the historic Rhine to Cologne, but from the car windows a fleeting glimpse was had of the scenic hills and castles, as well as the renowned Mouse Tower in the center of the stream.

At the time of this visit President John P. Lillywhite was presiding over the Netherlands Mission which included Belgium, and he and President Ballif, of the Swiss and German Mission, and David Lawrence McKay were in attendance at the Liege Conference. At the present writing President Lillywhite is again presiding in Holland, this being his third mission to that land. The special missionaries also met Elders Alvin Smith Nelson and Karl M. Richards, who were laboring in Liege. There is much to see in Brussels and in Paris, but little time was had for these cities.

More than twenty years before this world trip was undertaken Brother McKay labored in Glasgow, Scotland, and immediately upon setting foot on British soil he made a hurried trip to his old field while Brother Cannon visited the London Conference. The missionaries in England were laboring with fidelity but the people lacked the interest manifested in former years. A spirit of gloom and depression was apparent.

A royal welcome awaited the brethren at Mission headquarters in Liverpool. President Orson F. Whitney and his hospitable wife made the few hours spent with them most agreeable. They and Elder William A. Morton were on the pier to bid the two travelers "bon voyage" as the *Cedric* moved out to sea.

Since leaving home, these brethren had spent many days on the water. They had traveled on a great variety of vessels and had encountered all kinds of weather. Outwardly Brother McKay seemed to have become a really first class sailor, but he admitted, as they neared port, that inwardly, though not actually overcome by seasickness, he had not been really comfortable during any waking hour of the final trip. A world tour, therefore, is not all sunshine and pleasure.

The brethren had been stirred by the sight of colorful Japan, of the mammoth Chinese wall, of historic pyramids, the chaste Taj Mahal. But surpassing all else is the thrill which comes to an American when after a long absence he sees the inspiring Statue of Liberty at the entrance to New York harbor, and behind this his own native land.

Always interesting is the docking of a mammoth ocean liner at its pier. In close quarters, such as one finds in the Hudson, a large vessel is most unwieldy and must be shoved into its place by numerous small but sturdy tugs.

It is a trying period for people on deck who see loved ones waiting for them, but no amount of impatience can hurry the tedious process of landing. Not having any loved ones, or even friends as far as they knew, waiting for them on the pier the special missionaries were able to give their entire attention to the interesting sights.

Although unknown to them, Elder George Ashton, Jr. was there to meet the travelers and conduct them to the Mission Home, presided over by Brother and Sister George W. McCune. However, it was first necessary to pass the custom officials, a duty which, in the opinion of most Americans, robs homecoming of much of its sweetness. These troublesome but necessary officers are stricter in the United States than anywhere else in the world. It is not enough to open one's satchel or trunk and have the investigator look into it perfunctorily and close it again, as is usually done in European countries. First of all the traveler must make a declaration of everything purchased abroad and with its price. With this paper before him the officer usually goes through everything, sometimes dumping the contents of a trunk onto the tables and carefully inspecting every article. Woe to him who has something which has not been declared. However, Brother McKay's party had no serious trouble and very little delay.

During a large part of this tour, the brethren had been completely out of reach of their families. Any of their loved ones might have been dead for several weeks before word could have reached them. This in itself was sufficient cause for gratitude that they were again within telegraphic reach of home.

In Chicago a short visit was had with President Winslow Farr Smith, now president of the Ensign Stake, who then was in charge of the Northern States Mission.

The welcome accorded the missionaries by President Grant and his associates was at a nature to make their hearts rejoice. They were given to understand that their mission had been completed to the satisfaction of those who had called them.

During this trip which required 366 days, the missionaries traveled on 24 oceangoing vessels. They spent the equal of 153 days on the water, traveled a total of 61,646 miles not counting trips made by auto, streetcars, tugs, ferryboats, horseback, camels, etc. Of the miles traveled, 23,777 were by land and 37,869 were by water.

CHAPTER 25

THE MOST WONDERFUL THING ON THE JOURNEY

"Who can utter the mighty acts of the Lord? who can shew forth all his praise?"

—Psalm 106:2

Friends have frequently asked: "What was the most wonderful thing you saw on this journey around the world?" The brethren usually answer by enquiring, "What in your opinion is the most wonderful thing to be seen on such a trip?" Of course the answers are many and varied. The Chinese wall is often suggested. Stretching from the sea at Shanghaikwan inland for about fifteen hundred miles, equal to the distance from Salt Lake City to Chicago, it is indeed a structure which inspires wonder.

As has been stated, an engineer once estimated that it contained enough material to build a wall six feet high and two feet wide which would encircle the globe at the equator. It has stood for more than two thousand years, and one wonders how the stupendous task of building it was ever completed. The purpose of the wall was to keep out the hordes of invading Tartar tribes, and in the days prior to heavy artillery it must have been impregnable. But to it the credit of being the most wonderful thing cannot be given.

Perhaps then the greatest active volcano in the world, the mammoth Kilauea on the Hawaiian Islands, can be accorded the honor. One who has had the privilege of seeing this lake of fire, a veritable Hades of boiling and hissing lava, of hearing the sputtering and rumbling and roaring which it emits, can certainly imagine nothing of its kind which would be more impressive or unforgettable. But no, we must seek farther for the most wonderful thing.

One ventures to suggest the pyramids of Giza. These monster structures have stood for thousands of years and are rated by everybody as being among the world's wonders. How the 2,300,000 blocks of stone averaging three and a half tons each, which went into Cheops, the largest of the pyramids, could be assembled so early in the world's history still remains a mystifying problem. From the summit of one of these monstrous structures, a view may be had whose equal is not easily found. With the inscrutable Sphinx near its base, the fertile Nile valley to the east, and otherwise almost surrounded by the barren Libyan desert, with the memory of interesting or tragic historical events which have occurred in the vicinity, this view alone would compensate for a world trip if nothing more were to be seen. To this land Abraham, father of the faithful, came. Here Joseph, interpreter of dreams, saved Egypt and proved a savior also to his father's house. Almost at one's feet, Moses, the great leader and lawgiver, was born and grew to manhood. Here the children of Israel served until the Lord miraculously led them across the Red Sea. To this land the prophet Jeremiah is said to have come and here met death. In fancy one can see Joseph and Mary and the Holy Child toiling painfully over dusty plains to escape Herod's jealous wrath. But the inquirer must be told that this is not the feature of the world trip which will remain longest in memory.

Perhaps it was the ruins of the Temple at Baalbeck. High in these ruined walls are stones more than sixty feet long and thirteen feet wide and estimated as weighing not less than two hundred tons, and these are morticed into the stone beneath, and the stones above are morticed into them with an astonishing skill.

Or it may have been the Taj Mahal, that wondrous dream in white marble erected in Agra, India, at such cost of time and treasure, by the Emperor Jahan something more than three centuries ago. When one looks upon this structure and thinks of what mortals can do, it is easy to believe in the omnipotence of God. If mansions in heaven are to exceed this in splendor, they are indeed worth all man's effort.

Or if none of these, then it must have been Bethlehem or Calvary.

Now the inquirer is approaching the answer, but has not yet reached it; for as man now attempts to measure the sanctity of the simple manger by the coat of the gold and silver which adorn it, and evaluates Calvary by the diamonds and other so-called precious stones which cover it, so also has man for a price bedecked Christianity, so beautiful in its simplicity, with glittering ceremonies originating in human minds until the precious teachings of our Lord are well nigh obliterated.

No, the most impressive thing these missionaries saw was not the Chinese wall, nor pyramids, volcanoes, marble halls, storms at sea, nor even, and one says it reverently, Bethlehem or Calvary.

It was the spirit of Christ manifested in the preparatory work being done by the Church. He is coming to reign; and his coming as King of Kings, announced to the world by our Elders, will be infinitely greater than his simple birth or his cruel death. This spirit prompts men to sacrifice their personal interests in order to help prepare the way. It causes a feeling of brotherhood among peoples of different color and language and custom. In other words, the most wonderful thing in the world is the Gospel of the Lord Jesus Christ, unadorned and unadulterated. Perhaps some little space may be used in explanation. And as space is limited, reference can be made to but a few instances and with utmost brevity.

In Peking, with its million inhabitants, the special missionaries were divinely directed to the one suitable place in the city where the dedicatory prayer could be offered. On that day the Lord gave unmistakable testimony that he accepted what had been done and that this benighted people, comprising a quarter of the earth's inhabitants, would in due time hear the saving message. No less an authority than Ambassador Charles R. Crane stated that this Church could make a wonderful contribution to that afflicted country. The assurance came forcefully to the brethren that China, land of floods, droughts, famines, of pestilence and of revolution, will emerge from chaos and the sun of truth will rise upon her.

Let the reader recall that when the brethren went to the Pacific Islands, they were total strangers to the Islanders. These were of a different race, color, and language and with strange habits of dress and manners. There was but one thing in common: the Gospel, but that is destined to unite all mankind, regardless of all else. On this trip its power to do so was marvelously manifested, more even among the Polynesians, where racial differences are the greatest, than among the whites, if such a thing is possible. The story has already been told of these dark-skinned, scantily-clad people falling on their knees and kissing and bathing in tears the hands of the brethren at Sauniatu, on the Samoan Islands. And the visitors were no less moved. Their tears also were shed in bidding farewell to simple souls whom they had never met until a few days previously.

This same spirit of oneness was abundantly manifest with Elders met in fifteen different missions, though in most cases missionaries and visitors had never met previously. Furthermore, is anything more remarkable than to find hundreds of young men foregoing the association of loved ones, paying their own way, remaining clean despite alluring temptations, and finding unspeakable joy in such service?

In connection with this trip many prophecies were made and all were literally fulfilled. That is an indisputable, not an imaginary fact. One fulfilled prediction might be attributed to chance, but when the number grows into more than a dozen, what explanation can be offered?

Mention has been made and might be repeated of the way our travelers obtained passage on vessels which were already filled. So frequent were occurrences of this kind that none but ingrates would fail to give the Almighty credit for preparing the way. If there was nothing supernatural about it, why should these remarkable things occur to them times without number and not to other travelers whom they met?

When the angel Moroni visited the unknown youth in Palmyra, he said that the name of Joseph Smith should be known for good and evil throughout the earth. In eastern and western, northern and southern lands, the brethren saw the fulfillment of this prediction. Often the words "Mormon" or "Joseph Smith" brought a smile of derision to the lips of those who heard it; and occasionally it led to open and in some cases violent abuse. This occurred in the Antipodes and, indeed, in all parts of the world. On the other hand, people were met in all climes who gratefully acknowledged God's goodness in revealing to them that Mormon and Joseph Smith were holy prophets who, when every knee bows and every tongue confesses that Jesus is the Christ, will be recognized as having been chosen vessels.

In view of these and innumerable unmentioned things the assertion is again made that the spirit of the Gospel of Jesus Christ and its effect upon mankind is the most wonderful thing in the world.

A word in conclusion. It was not intended in the beginning to extend this account into a book of such size. The work has been done hurriedly at odd moments and in the midst of numerous pressing duties. Many important incidents have been overlooked, while often others less important have been mentioned. Perhaps an apology is due for the prolixity of the narrative, but like the elusive word "Amen" in some sermons, it has been difficult for the author to write

FINIS.

APPENDIX A

MAPS AND CHRONOLOGY

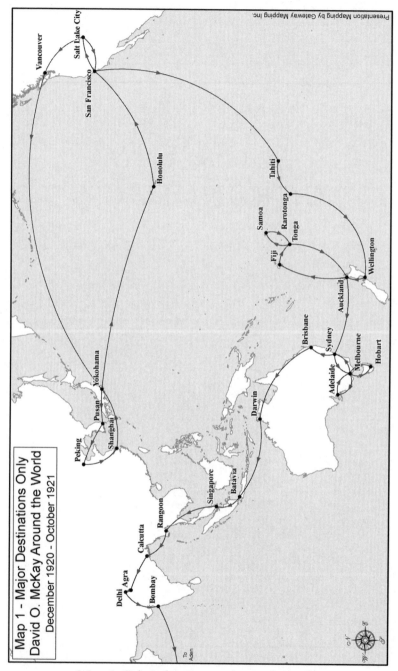

Map 1: Salt Lake City to the Arabian Sea

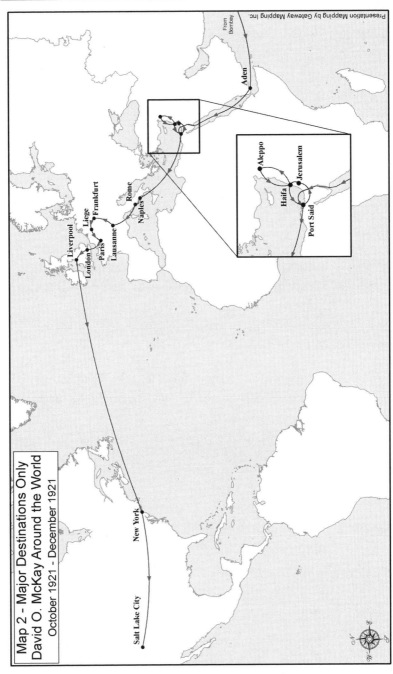

Map 2: the Arabian Sea to Salt Lake City

CHRONOLOGY

[Significant dates not described in this book are in brackets.]
A + following a date indicates more than one day was involved.

1920

CHAPTER 1:

Oct 14   Elder David O. McKay called to the mission.
Oct 15   President Hugh J. Cannon was asked to accompany Elder McKay.

CHAPTER 2:

Dec 2   Set apart for the trip in the Salt Lake Temple.
Dec 4   Left Salt Lake City for Vancouver, British Columbia, via Portland and Seattle.
Dec 7   Boarded the *Empress of Japan* for Yokohama via Victoria, British Columbia.

CHAPTER 3:

Dec 14-16 International dateline. Retired on the 14th and woke up on the 16th.
Dec 23   Yokohama, Japan.

CHAPTER 4:

Dec 24   Meetings in Tokyo, Kofu, and Osaka. Trip to the island of Tokyo. Trip to the island of Hokkaido aborted due to a storm. Trip to Nikko and return to Tokyo by train.

1921

Jan 1 + Meetings in Tokyo. Train from Tokyo via Kofu and Nara to Osaka. 14-hour express train from Osaka to Shimonoseki.

Jan 6 Shimonoseki, Japan, to Pusan, Korea, aboard the *Komo Maru*.

CHAPTER 5:

Jan 6 Pugan, Korea to Mukden, Manchuria, China.

Jan 7 Train from Mukden to Peking via Shanhaikuan.

Jan 8 Arrived in Peking (now Beijing).

Jan 9 Dedicated the land of China for the preaching of the gospel.

CHAPTER 6:

Jan 10 Met with the U.S. Ambassador in Peking.

Jan 11 Visited Great Wall of China.

Jan 14 + Train from Peking to Shanghai via Tienchin. Sailed on the *Tenyo Maru* from Shanghai, China, to Kobe, Japan, via Nagasaki. Train from Kobe to Osaka. Went to Kyoto with the elders working in that area. Train to Yokohama and Tokyo. Sailed on the *Tenyo Maru* for Hawaii.

CHAPTER 7:

Feb 4 + Arrived in Honolulu, Oahu. Spent 19 days in Hawaii.

Feb 7 Sailed to the island of Maui. Drove up Haleakala, and to Pulehu, where the previous conversion of 97 people took place.

Feb 8 [George Q. Cannon and Joseph F. Smith vision at the pepper tree. See Appendix B.]

CHAPTER 8:

Feb 9   Took the steamer *Mauna Kea* from Lahaina, Maui, to Hilo, Hawaii.

Feb 10   Conference meetings in Hilo.

Feb 10-11 Visited the Kilauea volcano overnight. [please refer to Appendix B.]

Feb 11 +   Returned to Hilo. Took a ship from Hilo to Honolulu. Took a steamer to Nawiliwili, Kauai. Visited the "Beach House" and "Spouting Horn." Returned to Honolulu for a missionary meeting. Attended Sunday School at Laie.

CHAPTER 9:

Feb 23   Sailed on the *SS Maui* from Honolulu for San Francisco.

Mar 1 +   Arrived in San Francisco. [Planned to secure passage to Tahiti on March 3rd.] Met by Pres. Grant, Pres. Ivins, Sis. McKay, and Sis. Cannon. Called back to Salt Lake for Pres. Lund's funeral.

Mar 4   Left San Francisco by train for Salt Lake City.

Mar 26   Left Salt Lake City by train for San Francisco.

Mar 29   Sailed from San Francisco on the *SS Marama* for New Zealand.

Apr 7   Crossed the equator; both missionaries initiated.

Apr 9   Arrived at Papeete, Tahiti.

CHAPTER 10:

Apr 10   Departed from Papeete on the *SS Marama*.

CHAPTER 11:

Apr 12   [Anchored off Avarua, Rarotonga in the Southern Cook Islands.]

Apr 13   Went ashore and took a ride around the island.

Apr 13   Sailed on the *SS Marama* at 9 p.m.

CHAPTER 12:

Apr 21   Arrived in Wellington, New Zealand.

Apr 22 +   Train to Huntly in the Waikato district. The "Hui Tau" conference was held for four and one half days.

CHAPTER 13:

Apr 27   [Train from Huntly to Auckland, New Zealand.]

Apr 30   [Departed New Zealand for Fiji on the *Tofua*.]

May 5   Arrived in Suva, Fiji.

May 6   Left for Tonga and Samoa on board the *Tofua*.

May 8 +   Nukualofa on the island of Tongatapu in the Tongan Islands. Passengers quarantined on ship because of a measles epidemic ashore. Contacted, but couldn't meet with the Saints. From Nukualofa to Neiafu on the island of Vavua on the *SS Tofua*. Measles quarantine less strict. Met with the Saints through a picket fence. Left Neiafu and visited Swallow Cave on the tiny island of Otea.

CHAPTER 14:

May 10   Harbor at Apia on Tuesday evening. Remained on board overnight.

May 11   Ashore in long boats at Apia, the island of Upolu (Western Samoa). Celebrations and feasts all day. Four days of conference meetings at Apia.

May 18   [Visited the graves of three Hilton children as promised.]

CHAPTER 15:

May 20   Left Apia in a small gasoline launch, the *Marstal*; 16 hours = 90 miles.

May 21   Arrived in Pago Pago on the island of Tutuila, American Samoa.

May 22 +   Visited the church coconut plantation and school at Maupusaga.

May 25   Left for Pago Pago. Met with the governor of American Samoa.

May 27   Left Pago Pago on the *Marstal* and returned to Apia.

CHAPTER 16:

May 28 +   20-mile horseback trip from Apia past Fusi to Sauniatu. Three days at the church plantation and the largest church school in Samoa.

May 31 +   Blessed the people at Sauniatu, Samoa. (Monument there now.)

Jun 6   Left Apia for New Zealand on the *Tofua*.

CHAPTER 17:

Jun 11   Elder McKay stopped at Nukualofa, Tonga, and was quarantined so he could visit the Tonga Mission.

Jun 11 +   Pres. Cannon went on to New Zealand to conduct some business there.

Jun 22   [Elder McKay was released from quarantine.]

Jun 24 +   [Elder McKay began visit to Tongan Mission.]

CHAPTER 18:

Jun 15   Pres. Cannon was guest at the mission home in Auckland. He investigated the cost of a schooner, and met with the Saints.

Jun 28   Pres. Cannon took train to Rotorua, the Yellowstone of New Zealand. President and Sister Taylor accompanied him.

Jul 1   [Pres. Cannon left Rotorua for Auckland. Elder McKay
            left for the northern Tongan islands.]

Jul 11   [Pres. Cannon tracted.]

Jul 18   Elder McKay arrived in Auckland on the Tofua; together
            again. Visited most of the districts in the New Zealand
            Mission.

Jul 25   [Train trip to Wellington (the capital), Hastings, and
            Korogatu.]

Aug 2   [Left from Auckland, New Zealand, for Sydney,
            Australia, on the *Ulimaroa*.

CHAPTER 19:

Aug 7   Arrived in Sydney after terrific storms.

Aug 9 +   Jenolan Caves near Sydney. Meetings in Sydney.

Aug 11 +   Took the train to Melbourne. Held meetings with
            missionaries.

Aug 15 +   Took boat to Hobart, Tasmania. Met with missionaries
            and spoke at town hall. Returned to Melbourne.

Aug 19   Left Melbourne for Adelaide by train.

Aug 22-23   Adelaide to Melbourne.

Aug 24   Arrived in Sydney. Elder McKay and Bro. Rushton went
            by rail to Brisbane via Newcastle. A short reception with
            the Saints at a brief stop in Newcastle.

Sep 3   Pres. Cannon left Sydney aboard the *SS Marella* for
            Brisbane.

Sep 5   The final meeting of the mission was held in Brisbane.
            This was the last organized mission they were called to
            visit. Visited all the Branches of that mission (except
            Perth) during a month-long visit. [They still had to
            deliver money to the Armenian Saints in Syria.]

Sep 6   Boarded the *SS Marella* at Brisbane en route to Java.

Sep 9   Townsville, Australia—no members.

Sep 16   Stopped at Darwin, Australia.

CHAPTER 20:

Sep 18   Left Darwin, Australia (the last stop in Australia).

Sep 25   Short Visits to Surabaya and Batavia (now Jakarta), Java. Batavia, Java to Singapore took 40 hours on the *SS Marella*.

Sep 27   Singapore ended their 24 days on the *SS Marella*. Went sightseeing for two days in Singapore.

Sep 30   Left Singapore on the *Arankola* for Calcutta, India. Pres. Cannon had terrible pain, but was healed by the Lord.

Oct 3   Stopped at Rangoon, Burma.

Oct 4   Left Rangoon.

CHAPTER 21:

Oct 6   Landed at Calcutta, India.

Oct 8   Took the 24-hour train ride from Calcutta to Agra.

Oct 9   Toured the Fort and Taj Mahal at Agra.

Oct 10 +   Took the train for the 3-hour ride from Agra to Delhi. [Did a little missionary work in Delhi.]

Oct 12   Took a 32-hour train ride from Delhi to Bombay.

Oct 13   Arrived in Bombay, India.

Oct 15   Sailed from Bombay, India, on the *SS Egypt* en route to Egypt.

CHAPTER 22:

Oct 20   Arrived and departed Aden on the Arabian Peninsula.

Oct 25   Suez and Port Said, Egypt. A 5-hour ride from Port Said to Cairo, passing through Zagazig.

Oct 26   From Cairo to Mena, the Pyramids of Giza, and the Sphinx. Visited the Tombs of Ti and the village of Sakhara. Visited the site of Memphis, where there is hardly a village now.

Oct 30   A train from Cairo to Kantara. Crossed the Suez Canal on a moveable "pontoon" bridge. A 15-hour train ride from Cairo to Jerusalem.

Oct 31   Arrived in Jerusalem.

CHAPTER 23:

Nov 2   Fighting in the streets of Jerusalem.

Nov 3   Prayed on the Mount of Olives. Visited Bethlehem. Took a car from Jerusalem to the Jordan River and the Dead Sea. Visited Jericho.

Nov 4   Took a train from Jerusalem to Haifa en route to Aleppo, Syria. Met President Booth (their guide in Syria) in the railroad station.

Nov 5   Took a car from Haifa to Beirut via Baalbeck (then Syria). Visited ruins of temple for worshiping Baal.

Nov 6   Took a train from Baalbeck to Aleppo, Syria; held meeting.

Nov 8   By car from Aleppo to Aintab; held meeting. Distributed the money collected for the suffering Armenian Saints. Major assignments from First Presidency completed.

Nov 9   Returned via car to Aleppo.

CHAPTER 24:

Nov 11   Aleppo to Damascus, Syria.

Nov 14   Damascus to Haifa by automobile via Tyre and Sidon.

Nov 15   [By auto to Sea of Galilee, Tiberias, Nazareth, and back to Haifa.] Last evening in Palestine spent on Mt. Carmel.

Nov 16   By rail from Haifa to Port Said in Egypt.

Nov 19-21   Pleasant Mediterranean cruise on the *Ormonde*. To Crete and between Scylla and Charybdis.

Nov 22   Arrived in Naples, Italy; a quick trip to Mt. Vesuvius and Pompeii.

Nov 23   [A long, tedious train ride from Naples to Rome.]

Nov 25   From Rome to Milan, and on to Lausanne, Switzerland.

Nov 26-28   Meetings. Lausanne to Basel, Switzerland.

Nov 29   To Frankfurt am/Main, Germany. Crowded meeting.

Dec 1   The Rhine River from Frankfurt via Mainz to Cologne, Germany.

Dec 2   From Cologne Germany to Liege, Belgium. Attended a two-day conference at Liege.

Dec 5   Express train to Paris, France.

Dec 7   Paris to London, England, via Calais, Boulogne, and Dover. Elder McKay took a side trip to Glasgow, Scotland. President Cannon stayed in London.

Dec 9   Left London for Liverpool.

Dec 10   Sailed from Liverpool to New York aboard the *Cedric*.

Dec 23   Arrived in Salt Lake City, Utah.

Dec 25   Elder McKay arrived home in Ogden, Utah.

APPENDIX B

SACRED EXPERIENCES

The author originally omitted these spiritual experiences from the manuscript, probably due to their sacred nature. They were subsequently made public by President McKay.

THE PEPPER TREE

While visiting Maui, the author expressed a desire to visit the spot where his father, George Q. Cannon, and Joseph F. Smith had a very spiritual experience many years before. The two missionaries visited that sacred spot accompanied by David Keola Kailimai, E. Wesley Smith, and Samuel Hurst. Brother McKay suggested they have a prayer. They found an old pepper tree to shade them from the hot sun, and Brother McKay was voice for the prayer.

Brother Cannon's personal journal includes this entry dated February 8, 1921: "I felt that I was treading on holy ground, that the veil between me and my father was very thin; indeed, I felt that there was no intervening veil. The brethren partook of the same feeling. We had prayers under a tree back of the building, and Brother Keola Kailimai says that while we prayed he saw two men shaking hands. He was surprised when he opened his eyes to see me standing with my hands at my side. I do not know the significance of what he saw, but I do know that Father and President Joseph F. Smith were there."

In telling of the experience the following year, Brother McKay said he told Brother Kailimai, "I do not understand the significance of your vision, but I do know that the veil between us and those former missionaries was very thin." Brother McKay then said, "Brother Hugh J. Cannon who was by my side, with tears rolling down his cheeks, said, 'Brother McKay, there was no veil.'" (See *Cherished Experiences from the Writings of President David O. McKay*, comp. Clare Middlemiss [1955], p. 52.)

THE VOLCANO

Near midnight on the evening of February 10, 1921, Brother McKay, Brother Cannon, and seven others left Hilo to see Kilauea, believed to be the world's largest active volcano. As they approached the volcano but were still several miles distant, they could clearly see its ghastly pale light dancing into the sky. They parked the car at the road's end and climbed the remaining distance to the top of the crater, arriving near 2 a.m.

What an unforgettable experience to witness the hissing and roaring sounds, the bubbling, burning, molten sea of lava, the sulphuric odor, and the brilliant shower of sparks shooting far into the sky. Words fail to adequately describe the impact on them.

Standing on the crater's rim, the observers experienced an unusual condition. The cold winds blowing against their backs caused them to feel chilled, while the heat from the crater's fiery cauldron burned their faces. One of the party found a ledge projecting from the crater's wall a few feet below the rim, where they could observe the spectacle while being protected from the chilling wind and the extreme heat.

Satisfying himself as to the ledge's safety, Brother McKay and a few others gingerly climbed down onto the ledge. They had been there for some time when Brother McKay suddenly said with alarm, "I feel impressed that we should immediately get out of here." No sooner had they climbed back up to safety than the entire ledge broke off and fell a great distance into the boiling lava. Those present all recognized this event as a manifestation of revelation given to a humble servant and a literal fulfillment of a priesthood blessing given to Brother McKay over two months earlier. (From Cannon family records.)

INTERPRETATION OF TONGUES

In an address given by President McKay to the BYU student body on October 8, 1952, he said: "The occasion was a conference held at Huntly, New Zealand, a thousand people assembled. Before that time I had spoken through interpreters in China, Hawaii, and other places, but I felt impressed on that occasion to speak in the English Language. In substance I said, 'I have never been much of an advocate of the necessity of tongues in our Church, but today I wish I had that gift. But I haven't. However, I am going to speak to you, my brothers and sisters in my native tongue and pray that you may have the gift of interpretation of tongues. We will ask Brother Meha, who is going to interpret for me, to make notes and if necessary he may give us a summary of my talk afterwards.'

"Well, the outpouring of the gift of tongues on that occasion was most remarkable. Following the end of my sermon Brother Sid Cristy, who was a student of the Brigham Young University, a Maori, who had returned to New Zealand, rushed up and said, 'Brother McKay, they got your message!'

"Well, I knew they had by the attention and the nodding of their heads during the talk. I said, 'I think they have but for the benefit of those who may not have understood or had that gift, we shall have the sermon interpreted.'

While Bother Melra was interpreting that or giving a summary of it in the Maori language some of the natives, who had understood it, but who did not understand English, arose and corrected him in his interpretation." (See "A Message for LDS College Youth," in *BYU Speeches of the Year 1951-53*, pp. 2-3.)

A SON'S TRIBUTE
TO THE AUTHOR

President Hugh Jenne Cannon
(1870-1931)

TWO EXCEPTIONAL MISSIONARIES

In 1920, David O. McKay was still a member of the Quorum of the Twelve Apostles of The Church of Jesus Christ of Latter-day Saints when he was appointed by President Heber J. Grant to undertake a historic mission to visit most of the foreign Church missions and potential mission areas around the world. His remarkable mission, chronicled in this book, was a significant step in the transition of the Church from a largely American and European church to its present status as a rapidly growing worldwide church.

My father, Hugh J. Cannon, was called to be Elder McKay's missionary companion. At Father's funeral, Elder McKay said, "I shall ever feel grateful to President Grant for having chosen Brother Hugh J. Cannon to be my companion on a special appointment to visit the missions of the world."

The outstanding life and great contributions of President McKay are well known and widely documented. Millions of us still hold him in loving remembrance. Therefore, no need exists to review President McKay's life here.

His missionary companion's Church assignments, on the other hand, were not as prominent or as widely known and appreciated. Furthermore, most of those who knew him personally and greatly admired him are no longer with us. It may seem strange to Church members that a General Authority was not chosen as Elder McKay's companion for such an important mission. Consequently, it seems appropriate to acquaint the readers with something of the background and spiritual stature of the author of this book. They should come to know more about his extraordinary character and faith. Such an insight should also help to understand and appreciate more fully the import of what he has written.

My sister and brothers have given me, father's oldest living child, the privilege of providing the readers with a sketch of his life. To us, he is something of a superhero. I could fill these pages with accounts of his loving kindness and humility as we experienced his companionship. However, I shall resist the temptation to do so, but will rely instead on his record and the opinions expressed by others.

Father was born January 19, 1870, in Salt Lake City, Utah, to George Q. Cannon and Sarah Jane Jenne Cannon. In his early life he experienced firsthand the intense persecution of the Mormon people. This prepared him to deal with persecution that he encountered later on his foreign missions. He wrote of the missionaries having to move about to avoid being apprehended and jailed. Mission headquarters had to be shifted for the same reason.

He honed his literary skills working at the publishing firm of George Q. Cannon and Sons, which was later donated to the Church and renamed Deseret Book Company. During his life he wrote two full-length novels and numerous editorials, short stories, and articles. He took down in shorthand and prepared most of the manuscript of his father's book *The Life of the Prophet Joseph Smith*.

Father's various Church positions provided a close association with many of the General Authorities. In addition, his father served in the First Presidency as First Counselor to three Presidents of the Church. Two of Father's brothers, a brother-in-law, and his father-in-law all served in the Quorum of the Twelve Apostles. Thus, in addition to his personal experience in presiding positions, he had unusual opportunities to observe and recognize firsthand how the dedicated selfless servants of the Lord are literally guided by revelation and inspiration in the Lord's restored Church in this day and age.

Father devoted most of his life in voluntary service for the gospel he loved. Serving the Lord was his first priority. He spent nine and a half years in the mission field. As if to test his faith, his mission calls seemed to come just when they would provide the greatest hardship and sacrifice.

He also served the Church in various capacities at home. When not on a formal mission, he devoted much time to stake missionary work, as well as teaching and serving as a set apart temple worker. He was made a member of the General Board of the Sunday Schools in 1896 and was the oldest member in point of service when he was released in 1924. He was a strong influence for good in the lives of the young people he taught in classes.

His first mission began in April 1891 in Germany, where he encountered severe persecution but was protected in miraculous ways. This mission was cut short by the death from the cholera epidemic of his brother David, who had also been serving a mission there. Father was released in November 1892 to accompany the body home.

He served on this mission without worldly resources or income. He later wrote: "We depended on the Lord for food and a place to sleep, and He did not forsake us. . . . I know that the man who puts his whole trust in the Lord and travels without purse and scrip will accomplish much more than one who has a regular allowance from home, and he will grow faster. The other brethren, seeing how they are outstripped, may become converted to the idea. As it is now, a man is prohibited from the blessing of preaching the gospel unless he has means."

During a later mission he wrote: "I can never return to Leipzig without having recalled to my mind the experiences I had in that city. Alone, unguarded and unwatched by any human being, without any organization or conferences, not asked to tract or do any other work, and never asked as to how I spent my time, the marvel to me is that I escaped the temptations which beset a young man in a large city. . . . I can go back to that city, and have always been able to go back, and look every man, woman, and child in the face without having to hang my head in shame."

In 1901 Elder Frances M. Lyman asked Father to accompany him on a mission to England. The particular work he wanted him to do was editing the *Millennial Star*. Father wrote: "I have been much surprised at the way President Lyman has asked my opinion about different matters, not only in regard to my mission here, but also in regard to other missions. I only wish I could live so that I could come up to his expectations."

After accompanying Elder Lyman on some tours of the European missions, Father was appointed to preside over the German Mission and put in charge of translating and printing the Book of Mormon and Doctrine and Covenants in German. The Swiss Mission was later combined with his German Mission. He presided there from July 1901 to March 1905.

Elder Heber J. Grant, who replaced Elder Lyman as president of the European missions, wrote Father of the importance of the new calling and said: "I . . . felt that you would be the most capable and devoted of any man for this office, among the many good brethren with whom I was acquainted. I assure you that you have my unbounded love and confidence."

Persecution raged on. The American ambassador reported that the German officials were determined to get rid of all Mormons. Despite the risks, Father continued his mission and even presented two handsomely bound copies of the Book of Mormon to the Kaiser and his queen!

Elder Richard R. Lyman, another member of the Council of the Twelve, wrote: "The Church has had in it no more fearless, no more courageous fighter for the cause of our Father in Heaven than Hugh J. Cannon. He was a man who knew no such feeling as fear. He was a glorious and remarkable son of a remarkable father. And with his courage and daring, he had unusual intellectual power. . . . His virtues are so outstanding and so numerous that I could write about him indefinitely."

Father wrote in his journal: "I have been a good deal discouraged over my inability to serve the Lord as I would like to. He has given me so much. In fact, I can hardly think of anything that I have ever asked Him for that has not been given me, and I would like to do more for Him, but it seems that I cannot. I cannot understand why I have always been put forward over men who are better and more able than I am. It frightens me, for I know that more will be required of me than if I had been left where it seems to me I belong." Those who knew him well would not agree with his humble self-depreciation. Later he wrote: "I can hardly understand why the Lord has been so good to me. He has answered my prayers in a marvelous manner, and I cannot but wonder at His goodness."

In 1904, while Father was still presiding over the Swiss-German mission, the Salt Lake Stake of the Church was subdivided into four stakes. He received word that he had been called as president of Liberty Stake, the largest of the four. It was not until his return in 1905 that he could be set apart for that presidency. He occupied that position for twenty-one years. In fact, he was not released during the mission with Elder McKay that is described in this book. Bryant S. Hinckley, his first counselor and father of President Gordon B. Hinckley, presided over the stake during his absence and succeeded him as stake president when he was finally released in 1925 to become once again president of the Swiss-German Mission, where he served for three more years.

Upon returning from that mission in 1928, Father was appointed first as associate editor and later managing editor of the *Improvement Era* magazine, where he served until his untimely death on October 6, 1931. President Heber J. Grant noted that Father was one of the few men he would trust to write and publish Church editorials without his personal review.

Elder Thomas E. McKay, brother of President McKay, was the visiting General Authority at one of our stake conferences. The theme of his talk was the loving bond which develops between a mission president and his missionaries as he had experienced it when presiding over missions. He also referred to the lovely mission home in Switzerland.

I spoke with him after the meeting and mentioned my nostalgia, having lived in that mission home from 1925 to 1928 as a boy. When he learned who my father was, tears actually welled up in his eyes as he said, "Your father was *my* mission president. He was the greatest mission president this Church has ever produced!"

In the transcript of Father's funeral, many heartfelt accolades were recorded. It has been difficult to limit the quotations. President Heber J. Grant said: "I have known Hugh J. Cannon from his childhood. I was reasonably intimate with him before he went upon his first mission, and labored side by side with him while I presided over the European Mission. I know of no more diligent, faithful, splendid missionary than Brother Cannon. I believe there is no place in all the world where men become so closely attached to each other as they do in the mission field. There is no labor, when it is performed under the inspiration of the Spirit of the Lord, that brings us nearer to our Father in Heaven and our Savior as laboring to bring souls to a knowledge of the truth. . . . There are few men who have done more in bringing souls to a knowledge of the gospel of Jesus Christ, the Plan of Life and salvation, with tongue and pen, than has Hugh J. Cannon."

President McKay said of him: "But the most impressive trait of his character as I found it during those thirteen months of constant companionship with him was his implicit faith in the gospel of Jesus Christ. There was absolutely no doubt in his mind about the existence of our Father in Heaven. Indeed during that trip we seemed very close to the Lord, as close as we have ever been in all our lives."

Father was able to accumulate and remember a vast and varied array of facts. Like his father, he was blessed with a phenomenal memory. Though he attended the University of Utah, he was really self-taught. An entry in his journal on his first mission states, "My main wish at present, next to filling a good mission, is to improve myself, that I may become an intelligent and useful man." He read a great variety of good books and observed the world about him at every possible opportunity. He knew, however, that knowledge needs to be applied wisely or it becomes a detriment.

President McKay described him as one of the wisest men he had ever known. At Father's funeral he quoted a tribute to "another great and good man" and said: "My friend is worthy of this and more. Brother Cannon was '. . . full at once of integrity and sagacity, speaking ever from the level of his character and always ready to substantiate opinions with deeds: a man without any morbid egotism, or pretension, or extravagance; simple, modest, dignified, incorruptible; never giving advice which friends did not endorse as wise; never lacked the virtue to bear calamities which resulted from his advice being overruled. Such a man could not but exact that recognition of commanding genius which inspires confidence.'"

It was not only General Authorities who appreciated Father. The president of the Samoan Mission wrote of a native member who, after counseling with Father during the world tour, said, "If the time ever comes when my life and welfare hang in the balance and where I might select a judge who would be absolutely fair, just, merciful, and unswayed from justice by any outside influence, that judge would be Hugh J. Cannon."

Father had an intense love for the beauties of nature and for fine music. He felt a Christlike love for all mankind, no matter what their condition or behavior. We get an insight into his attitude and philosophy as he wrote: "The world is very beautiful if one will only keep one's eyes open. No work of nature, no flower, no plant, no tree is without beauty. But our eyes are often closed. It is the same with mankind. It is difficult to imagine a human being who has not got some really fine traits of character. All are children of God, and all have in them something of the divine. This may be hidden by a rough exterior; it may be covered by rubbish or even filth. . . . A certain improvement could be brought about by improved treatment."

Perhaps the most outstanding quality that father exhibited, an outgrowth of his immovable faith, was an unusual humility and reverence for all things sacred. When it was necessary to use the Savior's name as in a prayer or ordinance, it was uttered in almost hushed tones of love and reverence. Otherwise he referred to the Savior as the Creator, Lord, or Redeemer.

AN EVERLASTING FRIENDSHIP

At Father's funeral Elder McKay spoke of their friendship: "Before that time I had a general acquaintance with him, but from December 2nd, 1920, until December 20th, 1921, Brother Hugh and I were together night and day, with but one short exception of three weeks when I went into quarantine at Tonga that we might visit the Saints in that mission, and he went to New Zealand to fill our appointment there. With that exception we were out of each other's company scarcely an hour during the thirteen months of that memorable tour. We were together under all kinds of conditions. We were in confidence, in prayer in the most holy places in all the world. Our hearts were opened to each other as seldom brothers of flesh and blood know one another.

"Actually then I must speak of him first as a friend. None truer, none more faithful in all this world. . . . This brother always in friendship lost himself for the good of others. In that as in every other phase of his life he was a true disciple of the Master who said, 'He that will lose his life for my sake shall find it.' Here was a man who did not hesitate under any circumstances to lose himself to comfort the least of God's children. . . . Oh, he was a friend, and always and everywhere a gentleman."

Father humbly recognized the great privilege and honor that came to him in his call to serve on such a special missionary journey. Despite the deep friendship and intimate brotherhood that Elder McKay and Father felt for each other, Father did not consider it appropriate to address his companion by his first name. It was always "Brother McKay" or "Elder McKay." He felt great respect and deference for those presiding over him in priesthood callings.

Their deep mutual respect and friendship did not diminish before Father's unexpected passing in 1931, and apparently their association continued even beyond that worldly separation!

President McKay passed away one day before the 100th anniversary of Father's birth. I like to believe that President McKay just had time to be joyously welcomed and become acclimated to his new situation on the other side before joining Father in celebrating the century since his mortal birth.

The Mormon Pacific Historical Society proceedings of 1991 contain references to some of the events which occurred during their missionary journey. They also refer to President McKay's second visit to Pago Pago on January 14, 1955. He spoke to a gathering of 746 Church members and said, "I can feel the presence of Hugh J. Cannon with me today."

My older sister, Constance Cannon Wilson, was sitting in the row behind President McKay's wife at the dedication of the Church's Los Angeles Temple in 1956. When he and his associates came down the aisle past her in preparation for the service, she strongly felt the presence of our father in the group. She mentioned this to Sister McKay. When the President joined his wife, she said: "Remember Connie Cannon? I think she should tell you about what she experienced." When Connie told President McKay that she felt her father's presence with him, he responded: "Of course you did, my dear. He was here with me."

A BOOK LONG DELAYED

While Elder McKay was presiding over the European Mission in 1923, he wrote Father: "I am sufficiently convinced of its importance to suggest that you and I assume jointly the responsibility of publishing that book." Mention is made in the preface of Elder McKay's desire to have the spiritual aspects of their mission published. The work progressed very slowly because both continued to carry heavy responsibilities.

Father was able to turn to his wife, Sarah Richards Cannon, for help in transferring the data from his missionary journal into a publishable manuscript as President McKay and Father had envisioned it. Her background equipped her ideally for that task. By the time of Father's death, they had been revising and polishing the manuscript with Elder McKay's continued encouragement. Thereafter Mother continued as best she could, but none of us were in a position to finalize it. However, it was fairly complete with pencil notes along the margins of corrections or suggestions.

When Elder McKay was called by the Lord to become His prophet and President of the Church in 1951, Mother felt it might be timely to consider publication of the manuscript. She made an appointment with the President to which I accompanied her. As he came out to greet us in the outer office, his secretary commented that their mission around the world must have been as important as the biblical missionary journeys of the Apostle Paul. The President added that if we understood its real significance, we would recognize it as even more important to the Church than Paul's missions.

President McKay still felt strongly that publication of this account was highly desirable but quoted, "I am the hero of my own diary." In true modesty he didn't feel it appropriate that he should be involved in its publication. He requested that we leave the only copy of the manuscript (we had no access to copy machines in those days) with a trusted publisher to determine the best way to have it published. The reaction there was favorable. In correspondence with President McKay, he wrote me, "If . . . you decide to publish it in a book I should be very pleased to write a foreword." Unfortunately, this was never to be.

Due to a change of personnel at the publisher, the manuscript was misplaced and lost for many years until well after President McKay's death. It eventually found its way into the archives at the McKay home. Finally, it was returned to our possession and again became available for publication.

George Richards Cannon

INDEX